THE ULTIMATE GUIDE TO
COOKING WILD GAME

RECIPES AND TECHNIQUES FOR EVERY NORTH AMERICAN HUNTER

JAMES O. FRAIOLI

Skyhorse Publishing

Visit our website at www.skyhorsepublishing.com.

10 9 8 7 6 5 4 3 2 1

Library of Congress Cataloging-in-Publication Data is available on file.

Cover design by Daniel Brount
Main cover photo credit: Tucker + Hossler

Print ISBN: 978-1-5107-5545-1
Ebook ISBN: 978-1-5107-5547-5

Printed in China

CONTENTS

INTRODUCTION

As hunters, we love to hunt. The *Sporting Shooters' Association of Australia* (SSAA) summarized it best when they said, "We gain a perfectly natural, deep-seated satisfaction from hunting all kinds of animals." From the darting little hare right up to the thundering Alaskan moose, and every other game animal in between, it's no surprise more than fifteen million people participate in hunting every year across America. However, hunting doesn't always mean killing. Sometimes we kill, and sometimes we don't. But on every occasion, the main aspect most of us enjoy is the hunt itself. To stalk in and check out a roaming black bear or a trophy elk, and then make the decision whether to take the animal without them knowing we're there, is an achievement on its own, from which we, the hunter, should feel a deep sense of satisfaction.

Today, according to hunters across the country who have been hunting their entire life, the passion to hunt remains and continues to grow. Having such a passion means hunters are able to share their experiences with their sons, daughters, nephews, and grandkids, as many of them will become proficient and ethical hunters in their own right. It's true many hunters never really understand why they feel so passionate about hunting, but perhaps the main contributing factor is in their genetic make-up. Ever since our ancestors all those eons ago started to hunt prey species after acquiring a taste for meat (protein), man has been a hunter. And now, even after all this time, the urge to hunt continues to be thoroughly engrained in our DNA.

Anthropologists agree that the protein in our ancestors' diets, derived mainly from animals they hunted for their meat, has played a major part in our evolution as a species and is the main factor for how our brains continued to grow as we evolved as a species. Just imagine where the human race would be today if our ancestors had not killed other animals for food.

From all those ages ago, right up until only a few generations back, it was normal everyday behavior for humans to hunt, mainly to feed their families, but also to satisfy a deep-seated need that could arguably be described as pleasure. There can be no argument that it is a pleasurable experience to do something you enjoy while providing for your family.

In *The Ultimate Guide to Cooking Wild Game*, you will find general information and hunting tips for twenty-five common North American game animals. The animals' origin, range, migration, and travel patterns, life-span, size and weight, typical habitat, and desired foods are included to further educate along with suggested hunting methods and reasons the particular animal makes for excellent table fare.

Statistics prove there are also many health benefits of consuming wild game meat. First, there is hardly any fat in wild game. If you have doubt, simply make a meatloaf with wild game and a meat loaf made with ground beef from the supermarket. The grease that pools in the bottom of the Pyrex dish when meatloaf is made with ground beef should be proof that flavor reigns supreme in wild game. The low-fat content from wild game can be attributed to the active lifestyle and natural nutrition of such animals. Secondly, you won't find hormones and antibiotics in wild game meat, which is one of the more significant benefits that compel more and more health-conscious carnivores to favor wild game. Wild game also has the edge when it comes to flavor. Exercise boosts blood circulation, which boosts flavor. So, an active, wild animal's meat is likely tougher than a less active, farm-raised animal's meat, but it's also packed with more flavor compounds. It's also worth noting that overcoming a tough cut of meat often means slow cooking. It's an easily accessible solution. Slow cooking gave us BBQ pork shoulders, and who's not in favor of that? Lastly, along with delectable flavor comes the benefit of essential fats like omega-6 and omega-3, which are critical components of a healthy diet. The mixture of fats found in wild game meat helps lower cholesterol and reduce other chronic disease risk. In the pages ahead, you will find seventy-five savory, easy-to-make recipes for cooking wild game. From Roasted Rabbit Chili (page 29) and Black Bear Meatloaf (page 53) to an Antelope Summer Salad (page 87) and Kung Pao Pheasant (page 137), each dish is also paired with a suggested wine to further enhance your dining experience among friends and family.

Experts in the field of anthropology from around the world anticipate that the instinct and urge to hunt and feast on one's kill will be with humans for thousands of years to come. Even though a great deal of "modern humans" don't actually hunt at all and have not had to do so for many generations, we can expect hunting as an instinct to continue rising to the surface in modern humanity.

In some instances, man appears to have gone from the once mighty hunter/gatherer to little more than a scavenger. It could be argued that, in some respects, modern humans have actually started to devolve. How many people do you know who are happy to eat meat from the supermarket where they do their hunting and gathering, but would give us a hard time for killing our own game meat? Plenty of them are out there, willing to scavenge their meat from someone else—someone they contracted to do the killing for them—and that's perfectly acceptable as long as they respect our right to do it ourselves.

So, good hunter, rejoice in the knowledge that the hunting we do is a normal and natural, biologically human behavior, whether we hunt animals on dry land or hunt fish in the rivers or oceans. Whether we hunt for food, for pleasure, or for environmental management, know we are just reacting to an innate human instinct that has been with mankind and our predecessors for hundreds of thousands of years and one that will be with us for many more years to come. The fact that we gain pleasure from hunting and fishing is something that we should all take pride in. As the noted Spanish philosopher Jose Ortega y Gasset stated: "One does not hunt in order to kill, on the contrary, one kills in order to have hunted." Enjoy the hunt, as well as the taste and flavor of your successes!

FIELD DRESSING EQUIPMENT— SMALL AND LARGE GAME

Once you have successfully identified and targeted your specific game, thanks to the insights of this book, the real work will begin if you have downed your animal. For small game and birds, the task isn't terribly daunting, but field dressing an elk or moose and packing out 100 or 200 pounds of meat along with your gear takes considerably more effort. To help make your haul-out as easy as can be, below is a general list for what you should carry on your next hunting trip to properly field dress your game. To make the task *even easier*, hunt with a friend, which allows for a much more efficient and safe process for packing out the meat.

MARKING TAPE

Marking tape, particularly photodegradable tape that breaks down over time when exposed to sunlight, is good to have on hand when your shot isn't perfect. Rather than dropping in its tracks, a wounded animal, as the result of a bad shot, may run for twenty yards or two miles. Having a roll of tape on hand will allow you to mark the track of the injured animal (via blood, hair, etc.) rather than trying to remember the location of those signs, especially if you're hunting in thick vegetation or near dark.

CUTTING TOOLS

Hunting Knife:

This can be as varied as you'd like, from a classic folding hunting knife to elaborate knives with replaceable blades. It's good practice to have a bright handle on your knife, like blaze orange. This makes your knife much easier to find, especially when buried in the animal or in vegetation.

Knife Sheath:

A sheath protects your knife and yourself when the blade is not in use. Always good to have on hand.

Sharpener:

A must when cutting up your bounty. Always make sure your knife is razor sharp before using. If you prefer a knife with replaceable blades, plan for 1 or 2 blades per animal, and maybe another to keep on hand as a spare.

Gut Hook:

This tool quickly cuts through thick skin, saving your knife's blade for the meat. However, a sharp knife will work just fine, especially when you're packing your gear in and out and weight is of the utmost importance. If you opt for a gut hook, select a lightweight model.

Bone Saw:

Not necessary, but some hunters prefer to carry one. All depends on your method of field dressing.

OTHER EQUIPMENT

Cords or Rope:

Handy for hanging meat to cool while making trips out or filling other tags.

Game Bags:

Game bags are ideal to keep your meat clean and cool when packing out in the field. In a pinch, you can use pillowcases.

Gloves:

Those blue disposable Nitrile gloves are inexpensive while keeping your hands clean and warm. Figure a couple pairs per animal.

Ground Cloth:

Whether you're using a nylon tarp or an old bed sheet, a ground cloth helps keep your meat clean and out of the dirt.

Light-Weight Sled:

Great when field dressing in deep snow. A sled definitely makes it easier to transport the weight and haul out, especially heavy loads. If there's a place you can stash the sled close by while hunting, even better.

Pack Liners:

The 2mm- or 3mm-thick trash compactor bags work well to line your pack and bags to prevent blood and stains from ruining your gear. Pack a couple for field dressing and keep a couple extra in your vehicle.

Zip Ties:

Great for many uses, such as connecting your hunting license to your game while field dressing.

FIELD DRESSING EQUIPMENT— WILD GAME BIRDS

Always check the regulations regarding the field dressing of waterfowl and game birds in the state you're hunting, as regulations vary from state to state. For example, some states require that the head and a wing remain on waterfowl to determine the sex and species while in other regions you may have to leave the head on a cock pheasant.

PLUCKING VERSUS SKINNING

Many hunters prefer to pluck their upland birds and skin their waterfowl. The decision is entirely up to you. Both types of game birds can be plucked or skinned. Plucking your birds leaves the skin on and makes for a tastier meal by sealing in natural juices, but it may leave annoying pinfeathers or down. Skinning, meanwhile, allows you to clean your birds faster and makes it easier to remove the heavy fat under the skin that adds an oily taste to the meat. However, it's often difficult to keep the meat moist while cooking.

EQUIPMENT

When field dressing game birds, there isn't too much equipment and tools involved, as opposed to field dressing large game like elk or moose.

Sharp Hunting Knife (with sharpening stone or replaceable blades and sheath):

As noted previously, in the small and large game field dressing equipment list, a sharp hunting knife is a must, especially when removing the bird's head, feet, and wings, and then gutting the animal.

Snipping Shears or Scissors:

This tool is useful for cutting off wings and legs of larger birds such as geese, ducks, and turkeys, but isn't essential.

OTHER EQUIPMENT

Game Bags:

Small game bags are ideal to keep your birds clean and cool when packing out in the field. In a pinch, you can use pillowcases.

Gloves:

Again, blue disposable Nitrile gloves are inexpensive while keeping your hands clean and warm. Figure a couple pairs depending on how many birds you are cleaning.

Ground Cloth:

Whether you're using a nylon tarp or an old bed sheet, a ground cloth helps keep your birds clean and out of the dirt.

Pack Liners:

The 2-mm or 3-mm-thick trash compactor bags work well to line your pack and bags to prevent blood and stains from ruining your gear. Pack a couple for field dressing and keep a couple extra in your vehicle.

OPTIMAL WORKSPACE

Now that your field-dressed game is finally home, it's time to create the perfect workspace for butchering the meat. Ensuring the counters and work surfaces are clean and organized helps keep the process running smoothly and efficiently while also guaranteeing the meat is preserved to the best of your ability. The best cleaning products, from salt and lemon or vinegar and water, to more chemical-based cleaners and bleach, all have their part in keeping your surfaces sanitized. Using natural cleaners on wood is best, as it's porous; soaking a cutting board in lemon juice and salting overnight will prevent bacteria from growing quickly when using a board over the course of a day. Washing knives and tools when switching between cuts, and keeping surfaces wiped clean as you work will also keep your surface as clean as possible.

Sharpening knives and tools the day before you plan to butcher is good practice, as is keeping essential tools close at hand. Arranging your knives and tools in order of use, and from the most used to least used, is also important when butchering so nothing is far from reach. Wearing a designated apron or work coat also helps keep the area clean and prevents the transfer of bacteria to other areas of your kitchen or home. Washing your apron in hot water when changing types of meat, as well as when you're finished for the day, will also keep bacteria from wandering and cross-contaminating.

Once your meat is wrapped and stored (information about this follows), disinfect all of your cutting boards, counters, and surfaces as if you're just beginning. Splatters can reach farther than expected, and keeping a kitchen clean is the foundation of ensuring that every meal is prepared to food-safe best practices.

Before butchering, dry or wet aging your meat is a best practice to ensure that the connective tissue has had a chance to break down and the muscle fibers have had time to denature. It's also important to ensure that the meat stays a consistent 34°F to 37°F for the days or weeks that the meat ages. Wet aging is usually easiest for the home butcher, as the wet aging process happens after the meat has been butchered and allowed to thaw. Keep the meat in its vacuum-sealed bag for up to two weeks after it's removed from the freezer. Dry aging requires larger hanging spaces, as the meat needs to be hung in large pieces before the butchering and preserving process is finished. This is easy for a commercial butchery with a walk-in fridge, although most home butchers don't have that luxury.

PROPER PACKAGING AND STORAGE

Vacuum-sealing meat, especially poultry, rabbit, and smaller game, is preferable, as it prevents meat from being exposed to the air for long periods of time. Freezer-burned flesh doesn't cook well and has an unsatisfactory taste, and all of the natural moisture from the meat has evaporated. Vacuum-sealing is also preferable for larger cuts of game if wet aging is desired, although this method can be challenging because excess liquid in the vacuum bag can ruin the seal. Otherwise, for large cuts of meat, butcher paper works perfectly well. Wrapping the meat twice prevents freezer burn and is also much more economical when working with larger animals.

Using a Sharpie-style marker will ensure that dates don't freeze off and won't bleed through to the meat. Write on the paper or bag before the meat is added—temperature changes can cause the marker to smudge before the ink is set. Always use freezer tape or string to close the packages; masking tape or duct tape will come loose in the cold freezer. On each package, write the cut of meat, date and use-by date, as well as any additional storage information or what you'd like to use the meat for ("beef strips for stir-fry"). This will help prevent mystery meat from appearing a year later and cuts going unused at their optimal time.

When storing meat in the refrigerator, place in a bottom drawer. This keeps other fresh ingredients in your refrigerator safe and clean from any bleeding or dripping and ensures a more consistent and cooler temperature. Keeping the same labeling system and rotation in both the refrigerator and the freezer is also a best practice.

REFRIGERATOR AND FREEZER SPACE

Labeling and creating your own best practice system for storage in the refrigerator and freezer is important to ensure nothing goes to waste. Place cuts of meat that need to be used first on the top right of the freezer and larger cuts in the bottom left. Rotating through your meat helps prevent freezer burn and the inevitable reality of losing cuts to the bottom of the freezer. Packaging by portion size, based on your family's typical eating habits, guarantees that what is thawed will be consumed. Erring on the side of smaller package portions—for example, two steaks are better than six—is best practice so you don't thaw more than you need that day.

How long should meat be kept in the refrigerator or freezer?

Different cuts of meat often determine the amount of time it can safely be stored in the refrigerator or freezer. For maximum quality, steaks and roasts, along with those smaller cuts for stir-fry and kabobs, should be refrigerated no more than 3 or 4 days; in the freezer, no more than 6 to 12 months. For ground meat, 1 or 2 days in the refrigerator or 3 to 4 months in the freezer.

Should you want to store your cooked wild game leftovers, figure 3 or 4 days in the refrigerator or 2 to 3 months in the freezer.

For cured meats and game sausages, it's best to only store in the refrigerator for about 1 week. It is not advised to freeze these cured cuts, so try to prepare only the amount you intend to eat within the week.

DEFROSTING AND FOOD SAFETY

Finally, the time has come to feast on the meat you have worked so hard to obtain. To make your experience as best as it can be, follow these general guidelines for defrosting and handling your stored game.

For the best quality, defrost the meat you intend to use in the refrigerator, never at room temperature. Simply place the frozen package on a suitable plate or tray to catch any juices and place in the refrigerator.

Defrosting times in the refrigerator (set between 35°F and 40°F) vary depending on the cuts of meat you're defrosting. If you have very small cuts or strips for, say, stir-fries and kabobs, defrosting in the refrigerator for 24 hours should yield a proper thaw. For ground meat and steaks, 12 hours or overnight should do the trick. According to the USDA, ground meat can be defrosted in the microwave if it's cooked within the same day, but microwave defrosting is not encouraged. If you plan to defrost small roasts or chunks of meat, figure about 3 to 5 hours per pound for a proper thaw. Large cuts and roasts can take up to 4 to 7 hours per pound.

KEEPING IT CLEAN

To avoid cross-contamination and prevent foodborne illnesses while defrosting or handling your defrosted game meat, the following best practices are advised:

- Wash your hands well in hot, soapy water before and after handling raw meat and other fresh foods.
- Keep raw meat and meat juices away from other foods, both in the refrigerator and during preparation.
- Wash all utensils, cutting surfaces, and counters with hot, soapy water after contact with raw meat.
- Keep carving boards separate from other food preparation areas and serving platters.

What about upland birds, waterfowl, and other forms of poultry?

Like chicken, the handling of your game birds is equally as important. Learning how to properly defrost birds only takes a few moments. Many say proper defrosting won't only make your meal taste better, but it will ensure you feel good after eating it. And this statement is important. Foodborne illness is dangerous, and birds, like chicken, have the potential to make you sick if not handled correctly. According to the USDA, the strains of bacteria most likely to be found on raw poultry are: *Salmonella, E. coli, Staphylococcus aureus,* and *Listeria monocytogenes.*

Practicing proper thawing methods and cooking poultry to an internal temperature of 165°F (74°C) will considerably reduce your risks.

To properly defrost your frozen game birds, never thaw on your kitchen counter. Bacteria thrive at room temperature.

Also, never rinse your frozen game birds under running water. This can splash bacteria around your kitchen, leading to cross-contamination.

To thaw your game birds correctly, and this is according to the USDA, the three suggested defrosting methods are:

Refrigerator:
This method requires the most preparation, but it's the most highly recommended. Birds like duck or a goose can take a full day to thaw, so plan your meals in advance. Once thawed, the birds can remain in the refrigerator for a day or two before cooking.

Cold Water:
For your frozen upland birds or waterfowl, place the bird(s) in a leakproof plastic bag. This will stop the water from damaging the meat tissue as well as any bacteria from infecting the food. Fill a large bowl or your kitchen sink with cold water. Submerge the bagged chicken. Change out the water every 30 minutes. This method should take 2 to 3 hours for a properly thawed bird.

Microwave:
This is the fastest method, but remember: Your birds must be cooked immediately after you thaw using a microwave. That's because microwaves heat poultry to a temperature between 40°F and 140°F (4.4°C and 60°C), which bacteria thrive in. Only cooking the birds to proper temperatures will kill the potentially dangerous bacteria. As mentioned previously, this method is not recommended and should be considered as a last resort.

Note: *According to the USDA, it's perfectly safe to cook poultry without thawing it. The drawback? The cooking process will take much longer—usually about 50 percent longer.*

MEAT AND WINE PAIRINGS

After the butchering process is complete and all your hard work is finally pulled from the freezer and properly defrosted, the second part of the story (and this book) begins. Preparing and enjoying all the delicious cuts of prized meat, from brining and marinating to quick searing and roasting—this book is filled with wonderful recipes, ideas, and suggestions graciously contributed by chefs, home cooks, and avid food bloggers across the country. Each dish is also paired with wine, a process that is an art unto itself.

A traditional rule of thumb: the color of meat should be paired with the like color of wine. This rule is a basic premise, although it doesn't always hold true. A rich, delicious elk tenderloin needs a wine to stand up to it, not something that will hide or disappear behind the flavor of the meat. Therefore, a Chardonnay or Riesling probably won't be the best to pair, while a Cabernet Sauvignon, Bordeaux blend, or Zinfandel would bring out the brightness and richness of the meat and complement perfectly. On the flip side, a tender rabbit loin would be overpowered by a rich, bold red wine, so a buttery Chardonnay would be delightful. Also, always consider the sauces and sides you're serving with the meal, as well, as this can also influence the perfect pairing. Quail in a richly spiced tomato sauce would pair exceptionally well with a Pinot Noir or Beaujolais Nouveau, while an antelope or wild boar tenderloin seared and served with an apple or fruit sauce would be better served by a sauvignon blanc or Gewürztraminer. Tasting the wine before serving and tasting the similar qualities between the dishes and the meat is the best way to ensure the pairing is ideal. Finding familiar grape varietals also helps ensure that your wine won't overpower the food and vice versa. The reality is, perfect pairings do enhance a dish, although the best wine is the one you like the most.

From hunting your favorite game animal and butchering the meat at home, to enjoying a delicious meal around the table, this book is a comprehensive guide to bagging your game and cooking the cuts you've stored, while sharing the experience among friends and family, over—what else? Of course, a wonderful glass of wine. *Salut!*

COOKING WILD GAME: ANIMAL PROFILES & RECIPES
SMALL GAME

HARE

Lepus

Hares (a.k.a. Jackrabbits) are a completely different species than rabbits. There are eight species of jackrabbits found in North America, including black-tailed, white-tailed, antelope, white-sided, snowshoe (the smallest hare, which is also known as the varying hare), Arctic tundra, and European. In general, their range spans across much of the western half of the United States and south into Mexico. These different species of hares can reach weights from about 4 pounds (black-tailed jacks) to 15 pounds (Arctic hares).

A hare's diet mainly consists of plant matter, wildflowers, a variety of weeds, seeds, vegetables, and fruit, with grass being one of the hare's most preferred foods. Some hares, like snow jacks, have peculiar eating habits in that they eat meat and fish, mostly during the winter.

Many hunters prefer shooting hares rather than cottontails because their large size provides more meat. There are several different ways to hunt hares, but the primary strategy is to hunt them with dogs. The most popular hunting dog breed for hares is the beagle. The large beagle, up to 15 inches at the shoulder, has little trouble tracking hares through deep snow, piles of brush, or heavy thickets and forcing hares out of the cover and past the hunter. Some hare hunters even prefer to use basset hounds or bluetick hounds, as they can keep up the chase with fast-running hares.

Other hare-hunting tactics include drives, still-hunting, and stand-hunting. Hares can be effectively driven from cover by a hunter. To employ this method, locate brush piles, thickets, or other types of thick cover. One hunter walks slowly through, stopping often to kick twigs and branches. The second hunter sets up in an opening away from the brush, waiting to shoot any hare bent on escaping. A 16- or 20-gauge shotgun is the ideal firearm for this strategy. Drives often produce a lot of fast action and anticipation—sometimes ending in laughter, as the hunters are left cussing at the hare that just escaped their plan unscathed.

Another hunting tactic is for a lone hunter to still-hunt for hares. Begin by looking for tracks and poop. Snow makes locating hare tracks a lot easier. Tracks usually lead to where hares are lying up. Generally, hares head for thick edge-cover in the hardwoods—places where hunters might look for grouse. Most times, these areas can be found in low-lying cedar swamps, the edges of beaver ponds, old grown-over fruit orchards, and other secluded places that provide food and cover from predators. A 12-gauge shotgun is an ideal firearm to use, as the hare usually escapes through a lot of thick cover.

Because hares nest above ground instead of using underground burrows, they tend to respond to danger differently than rabbits. Instead of seeking shelter underground, hares explode from their nest and, using their longer and stronger hind legs, run off at high speeds to escape danger. Jackrabbits and speed-jacks got their nicknames because of how fast they can run. They have been clocked at speeds ranging from 30 to 45 mph, and they can leap up to 10 feet at a single bound—making the hunting action fast and frantic on both dogs and hunters. Only keen reflexes and a dead-eye shot will consistently fill a hunter's game bag when shooting at fast-running hares.

Hare hunting with or without dogs requires a good set of snowshoes. In open terrain, some hunters even use cross-country skis. It also pays to dress in layered clothing, have waterproof foot-wear, warm gloves, hat, and insulated long-johns. A quality pair of sunglasses are a must when the ground is covered in bright snow.

Hare meat is considered red meat, like beef. It is dark in color, and its strong flavor tastes like the dark meat of other wild game. The legs always should be cooked with moist, slow-cooking meth-ods to help tenderize them. Hare saddles can be cooked rare. A hare can also be cut into five pieces (backstrap, two forequarters, and two hindquarters) or it can be cooked whole like a chicken. Hares can also be fried, baked, grilled, roasted, or slow-cooked. But, because of their strong-flavored meat, cooking methods can include full-bodied wines and dried fruits.

HARE BRAISED IN RED WINE

SERVES 2

1 hare, skinned, gutted, washed, and sectioned into 8 pieces

Marinade (see following page)

1 teaspoon small game spice blend, ground (coriander, black pepper, onion, juniper, pepper, pink peppercorns, cardamom, thyme)

Salt and black pepper, to taste

All-purpose flour, as needed

8 tablespoons clarified butter (or duck fat), divided

2 cups chicken stock

2 cups small yellow onions, peeled

2 cups button mushrooms

2 tablespoons balsamic vinegar

Italian flat-leaf parsley, optional, for garnish

In a bowl, add the hare sections and pour in the marinade. Cover and marinate in the refrigerator for 12 to 48 hours.

Remove the hare from the marinade, reserving the marinade, and dry the hare with paper towel. Season the hare with a teaspoon of small game spice blend, salt, and pepper, then dust each piece in flour.

In a Dutch oven, or large heavy pot, melt half of the butter over medium heat. Add the seasoned hare pieces, and brown on all sides. Note: You may have to do this in batches. Remove the pot from the heat.

In another pot over high heat, add the reserved marinade, along with the chicken stock. Bring to a boil, then lower the heat and simmer for 10 to 15 minutes, removing the residue from the surface. Pour the liquid through a strainer and add to the cooking pot with the browned hare.

Return the pot with the heat on low, cover, and simmer until the hare is tender (1 to 2 hours).

In a separate pan, melt the remaining butter, and add the small onions and mushrooms. Sauté until the onions and mushrooms are soft. Remove from heat and add to the pot with the hare. Add the vinegar and let simmer an additional 30 minutes before serving. Garnish with fresh parsley, if desired.

Continued on next page

Marinade

2 cups red wine

1 yellow onion, peeled and chopped

1 carrot, peeled and chopped

1 celery stalk, chopped

2 tablespoons wine vinegar

4 cloves garlic, peeled and chopped

1 tablespoon small game spice blend (coriander, black pepper, onion, juniper, pepper, pink peppercorns, cardamom, thyme)

To prepare the marinade, to a bowl, add the red wine, onion, carrot, celery, vinegar, garlic, and small game spice blend.

This recipe was adapted from the recipe by Épices de Cru & Spice Trekkers.

WINE SUGGESTION:

Clos Du Val Estate Cabernet Sauvignon

Clos Du Val was founded in 1972 on a dream to create the best Cabernet in the world. Their inaugural wine, the 1972 Clos Du Val Cabernet Sauvignon, was part of the group that topped French wines in the legendary 1976 Judgement of Paris blind tasting. Ten years later, their Cabernet Sauvignon took first place in the Judgement of Paris rematch. Clos Du Val's Estate Cabernet Sauvignon is full of dark red fruits, silky tannins, and a long, smooth finish, making it the perfect pairing for this meal.

WINE SUGGESTION:

Clos Du Val Hirondelle Vineyard Cabernet Sauvignon

Hirondelle is one of Clos Du Val's most prestigious vineyards located in the Stags Leap District of Napa Valley surrounding the winery. Clos Du Val's Hirondelle Vineyard Cabernet Sauvignon is rich in flavors of raspberry jam, toast, espresso, and fresh pastry. At 100% Cabernet, this wine shows nice tannin structure and a long-lasting finish, making it a delicious wine to enjoy with a special meal.

JUGGED HARE

SERVES 2

1 bottle (750ml) red wine

1½ cups beef stock

2 bay leaves

1 hare, skinned, gutted, washed, and sectioned

3½ tablespoons unsalted butter

1 yellow onion, peeled and diced

2 celery stalks, chopped

1 carrot, peeled and roughly diced

4 cloves garlic, peeled and crushed

1 teaspoon salt

6 black peppercorns

6 dried juniper berries

1 large sprig fresh thyme

2 teaspoons all-purpose flour

In a large bowl, add the wine, beef stock, and bay leaves. Stir, and add the hare. Marinate for at least 5 hours or overnight. Make sure the pieces of hare are fully submerged or turn them from time to time.

Remove the hare from the marinade, reserving the marinade.

In a Dutch oven (with tight-fitting lid), add the butter and melt over medium-high heat. Add the hare, and brown on all sides. Note: You may have to do this in batches. Remove the hare and set aside.

Add the onions, celery, and carrots to the pot, and sauté for 10 minutes, or until the onions are soft. Add the garlic and cook for a couple more minutes. Add most of the reserved marinade to the pot, reserving 5 tablespoons for later. Bring the mixture to a quick boil for 2 minutes.

Reduce the temperature to low and return the hare to the pot. While the hare is on a slow simmer, grind the black peppercorns and juniper berries in a pestle and mortar or a dry spice grinder. Add to the pot along with the salt, thyme, and bay leaves from the marinade.

Preheat the oven to 300°F.

Place the lid tightly on the Dutch oven and cook in the oven for 3½ hours.

Remove the Dutch oven from the oven. Remove the bay leaves and add the flour to the 5 tablespoons of reserved marinade and stir. Remove the hare from the oven and stir in the flour mixture to thicken the sauce a little before serving with the hare.

Adapted from the recipe by Rachel Walker.

SLOW-COOKED HARE STEW

SERVES 4

5 ounces prunes

2 ounces brandy

4 tablespoons brown sugar

1 tablespoon vegetable oil

2 hares

All-purpose flour, as needed, for
dusting

3 slices uncooked bacon

2 carrots

1 white onion, peeled and
chopped

1 celery stalk, chopped

1 clove garlic, peeled and
crushed

2 sprigs fresh thyme

1 bay leaf

½ cup red wine

1 cup chicken stock

Italian flat-leaf parsley, optional,
for garnish

4 cups cooked wild rice,
optional

Preheat the oven to 300°F.

Place the prunes in a bowl with the brandy and brown sugar. Stir
well and set aside to soak.

Heat a Dutch oven or heavy pot on medium-high heat. Add the oil.
Dust the hare pieces in flour and add to the hot oil. Sear the hare
until golden-brown on all sides. Note: You may have to do this in
batches. Remove the hare and set aside.

Add the bacon, carrots, onion, celery, garlic, thyme, and bay leaf
to the pot. Stir for 5 minutes, or until vegetables begin to soften.
Add the red wine and chicken stock. Return the hare to the pot
and add the soaked prunes. Cover and let cook for 2 hours, stirring
occasionally, until the hare is tender. Garnish with fresh parsley
before serving with a side of wild rice, if desired.

Adapted from the recipe by Good Food Magazine.

WINE SUGGESTION:

Clos Du Val Estate Pinot Noir

Clos Du Val's Pinot Noir vineyards are located in the southernmost part of the Napa Valley in a
region called Carneros. Carneros tends to be cooler in climate compared to other areas of Napa,
making it ideal to grow Pinot Noir. Clos Du Val's Estate Pinot Noir features bright red fruits like
strawberry and raspberry, finishing with a rich mouthfeel.

RABBIT

Leporidae

Hunters have been pursuing rabbits, particularly the Eastern cottontail, ever since the time of the earliest Native Americans. Although hunter numbers have declined from peak numbers, rabbit hunting still remains extremely popular overall and is one of the most popular small game pursuits across the eastern and south-central United States, as well as southern Canada. However, the dynamics of hunting cottontails have changed dramatically, and to achieve consistent success in the field, hunters must adapt to the new age of rabbit hunting.

Rabbits are found most anywhere they can find food sources and cover (for hiding from predators and also thermal protection from the elements). In most locations, sparse cover does not hold rabbits like it once did. Hunters must concentrate on areas with denser and more abundant cover to find rabbits in good supply. The absolute best locations for finding rabbits are areas with extremely dense cover. Gnarly tangles of briars, thorns, honeysuckle, and brush are difficult to reach for coyotes and foxes and make great locations for rabbits to hide from birds of prey. Likewise, they are hard to "kick up" by walking hunters. Rabbits hold much tighter in these areas and often do not jump unless almost stepped on or forced out by a rabbit dog willing to bury deep into cover. Having good rabbit dogs—especially one or two good "jump" dogs—is what often spells the difference in success these days.

"There he goes," is a common phrase shouted by hunters as the rabbit bolts from cover and streaks off down the field edge or across an open area to the next patch of thick cover. Hunters then try to determine which direction the rabbit is going and get in a position to intercept it and have a shooting opportunity when the rabbit circles back near the jump location. That part hasn't changed, but what has changed in many cases is how a rabbit runs and circles. Cottontails have a relatively small home range and are well familiar with their local surroundings. They do not like to leave this comfort zone. Therefore, a cottontail often darts out and puts as much distance as possible between it and the pursuing dogs. Then it slows down or stops and waits. As the dogs following the scent trail get near, the rabbit moves again. Eventually, it makes its way back to or near the original jump site. In areas where rabbits are constantly pressured by predators, especially along strips of cover between two crop fields, rabbits these days run much farther before turning and starting to circle.

Rabbit hunting is a tremendous amount of fun, and, of course, rabbits are one of the tastiest wild game meals to make an appearance on the dinner table. Time spent in the field, the camaraderie, and the "gourmet" dining experience all combine to make any extra effort well worthwhile.

The eating of rabbits and hares has a venerable history in Europe. Greeks, Germans, Spaniards, and Britons love rabbits and hares, as do Italians in certain regions. They also happen to be the building blocks of any true hunter's repertoire. At the table, these critters are often maligned as "poor people's food." Not true. Rabbit is far more interesting to eat than venison, is very tender, and of the perfect size. One rabbit will serve a person nicely, although you can split one rabbit between two people if you need to stretch things. To shine on the plate, rabbit needs to surround itself with ingredients and cooking methods that are more demure than, say, a heavy slathering of chilies, barbecue sauce, and tomatoes. Rabbits are also one of the few foods that really doesn't benefit from browning the way duck or lamb does.

Roasted Rabbit Chili

ROASTED RABBIT CHILI

SERVES 4–6

Olive oil, as needed

1 medium yellow onion, peeled and chopped

1 medium red bell pepper, seeded and chopped

1 medium green bell pepper, seeded and chopped

Kosher salt and fresh ground black pepper, to taste

4 teaspoons ground cumin

4 teaspoons ground chili powder

4 large cloves garlic, peeled and minced

1 (15-ounce) can whole plum tomatoes

1 (7-ounce) can diced green chilies

2 (15-ounce) cans beans of your choice (kidney, pinto)

2 cups chicken stock

2–3 cups leftover roasted rabbit meat, cleaned and chopped

Fresh cilantro, chopped, optional

Scallions, chopped, optional

Red onions, chopped, optional

Sour cream, optional

Tortilla chips, optional

Hot sauce, optional

Heat a medium saucepan over medium-high heat and add the olive oil. Add the onions and peppers, and cook until the onions are slightly translucent, about 2 minutes. Add a small amount of salt and pepper and the cumin and chili powder and cook 1 additional minute. (Note: Lower heat as needed to avoid burning.) Add the garlic and cook 1 additional minute. Add the tomatoes and green chilies and cook for 2 to 3 minutes. Add the beans and chicken stock, and bring to a boil.

Reduce heat to a simmer and cook for 1 hour. Add the chopped rabbit meat and cook 1 additional hour. Check flavor and adjust seasonings as needed, then serve with fresh cilantro, scallions, red onions, sour cream, crispy tortilla chips, and hot sauce of your choice, if desired.

Adapted from the recipe by Chef Raymond Southern.

WINE SUGGESTION:

Clos Du Val Estate Merlot

Clos Du Val has been growing Merlot since their start in the early 1970s, as it was a favorite grape of the founding winemaker, Bernard Portet. Clos Du Val's Estate Merlot has powerful aromas of raspberry, clove, and vanilla and is followed with flavors of black tea and ground coffee bean. Merlots typically have smoother tannins than other Bordeaux varietals, which makes this the perfect pairing for a chili dish.

PERUVIAN-STYLE RABBIT SLIDERS

SERVES 4

1 sweet potato, boiled until tender, peeled and set aside

Vegetable oil, for frying

Salt, as needed

Olive oil, as needed

1 small yellow onion, peeled and sliced

1 teaspoon ground cumin

Kosher salt and fresh ground black pepper, to taste

2–3 cups of leftover roasted rabbit meat, cleaned and chopped

½ cup chicken stock

1 tablespoon (or more) aji amarillo paste (available at Latin markets or online)

Slider buns (such as King's Hawaiian)

Lettuce

Tomato slices

Begin by preparing the sweet potato. Add about 2 inches of vegetable oil in a small pot over high heat. Slice the already cooked and cooled sweet potato. Lightly season with salt and fry in the hot oil until golden brown on both sides. Remove, set on paper towels to drain, and reserve.

In a large pan, sauté the onion in a small amount of olive oil until translucent. Add the cumin and salt and pepper and cook an additional minute. Add the rabbit and cook until just heated through. Add the chicken stock and cook until the mixture holds together well when placed in the slider bun. Just before serving, add the aji amarillo a little at a time until you reach the desired spiciness. Note: You can also add a little aji amarillo to your favorite mayonnaise and spread it on the bun before assembling the burger.

Toast the slider buns and assemble with lettuce, tomato, and the fried sweet potatoes.

Adapted from the recipe by Chef Raymond Southern.

WINE SUGGESTION:

Clos Du Val Estate Chardonnay

This Clos Du Val Estate Chardonnay is lean, polished, and elegant—a perfect accompaniment to a dish with so much spice and flavor. You'll find this wine has a nice acid structure with alluring mineralities on the finish, indicative of the region in which the grapes were grown, Clos Du Val's Carneros vineyards in South Napa Valley.

CHICKEN-FRIED RABBIT

SERVES 4

2 teaspoons baking powder

1 teaspoon baking soda

1 teaspoon black pepper

1 teaspoon salt

1½ cups buttermilk

1 egg

1 tablespoon Tabasco hot sauce

4 rabbit bellies, pounded and tenderized

Salt and black pepper, as needed

1 cup all-purpose flour, seasoned lightly with 1 pinch of salt, pepper, paprika, and cayenne pepper

Vegetable oil, as needed

In a bowl, whisk together the baking powder, baking soda, black pepper, salt, buttermilk, egg, and hot sauce. Set aside. This is your Chicken-Fried Rabbit Goo.

Lightly season the rabbit bellies with salt and pepper, then dredge in the seasoned flour mixture, followed by the Chicken-Fried Rabbit Goo. Repeat this process a second time.

Add some vegetable oil to come up to at least ¼-inch of a cast-iron or heavy skillet and place on a high heat. Once the oil is hot, quickly fry the rabbit bellies, turning once, until golden brown on each side (about 3 minutes per side), and let rest on a paper towel before serving.

Serve the Chicken-Fried Rabbit with coleslaw, country gravy, and mashed potatoes, if desired.

Adapted from the recipe by Chef Raymond Southern.

WINE SUGGESTION:

Clos Du Val Rose of Pinot Noir

Clos Du Val's Rose of Pinot Noir and fried chicken is a match made in heaven, so this fried rabbit pairing will no doubt also be a winning combination. Clos Du Val's Rose is made from 100% Pinot Noir grapes from their vineyards in Carneros, Napa Valley. It's thirst-quenchingly acidic, light, and refreshing with juicy notes of crushed raspberries and melon on the palate.

GRAY SQUIRREL

Sciurus carolinensis

The United States is home to five different types of squirrels: the gray, fox, flying (gliding), red, and ground squirrels. The eastern gray squirrel is the most hunted and dined-on squirrel of the two most popular squirrels (gray and fox). Both are hunted and prepared similarly.

The eastern gray squirrels (a.k.a. bushy-tail, squawker, nut-grabber, or tree-rat) are native to the eastern and mid-western United States. Gray squirrels have different fur colorings including brown, cream, tan, red, and even black. The black squirrel is a melanistic morph of the gray squirrel. Gray squirrels have the largest range. They inhabit a few eastern Canadian provinces, throughout the entire eastern United States, and Iowa, eastern North Dakota, Oklahoma, Kansas, and Texas. Within these areas, squirrels can be found most anywhere.

An eastern gray squirrel's primary diet includes buds, berries, seeds, mushrooms, corn, acorns and a variety of nuts. As most hunters know, squirrels love gnawing on dropped deer antlers as a source of minerals.

Gray squirrel habits are rather predictable but can be disrupted by foul weather. Squirrels are up and out at dawn for an early morning feeding at a choice nut tree or in a ripe corn field. They head back to their tree dens for a short squirrel-nap and head out again to feed in the late afternoon, always returning to the den as dusk approaches. Fox squirrels are the jumbo members of the squirrel family. They're late risers and feeders and head back to their nests earlier than gray squirrels. An adult fox squirrel can reach more than 2 feet from nose to tail and weigh as much as 2½ pounds! Its larger size provides more meat, making it top squirrel prey for hunters.

Hunters can enjoy a lengthy squirrel season for these abundant critters, generally from October to the end of March. Other than a small game hunting license and blaze orange hat or vest, this hunt doesn't require a lot of specialized hunting gear. Squirrels are generally hunted with 16-, 20-, and even .410-gauge shotguns or .22 caliber rifles. There are a few different standard methods used to hunt squirrels. The most challenging method is stalking (locating game and then getting close enough for a shot). It is a test of the hunter's woodsmanship skills. Other tactics include still-hunting, posting, using squirrel calls and, in some states, using squirrel hunting dogs.

Hunters will see and bag more squirrels if they hunt the two prime times of their movement patterns—just after dawn and in the late afternoon. Always try to get into position on wary squirrels by getting to your location before dawn. When temperatures begin to drop in winter, the best time to hunt squirrels is during the midday when it gets warmer. In an area where there are acorns and other nuts, sit at the base of an oak tree. Remain still and quiet while waiting for squirrel activity to begin.

Squirrels have excellent eyesight and equally keen hearing. *Stealth* is the key word when it comes to hunting squirrels. One wrong turn of a head or movement of a hand is all it takes to send squirrels fleeing, bringing the hunt to an instantaneous end. Patience and the ability to move carefully will always pay off in bagging a limit of gray or fox squirrels.

Squirrel meat is not gamey. Its unique flavor is light and has an earthy taste that is more subtle than rabbit. Its lighter colored meat is rather sweet and wonderfully textured, with a hint of nutty taste and aroma. It may be too cliché to say this, but squirrel meat is the one wild game that *does taste like chicken*. No, really, it does! The darker thigh meat, however, has the nuttiest and most tangy flavor—but not in a bad way.

One squirrel is usually enough to feed a single person. Squirrels can be prepared in a wide array of cooking styles. Squirrel meat is ideal in a casserole, stew, or in a slow cooker with vegetables. It is also a delightful tasting meal when baked, grilled, seared, or floured and fried. It can even be cooked whole over an outdoor campfire on a spit. Basically, it can be prepared in any way that chicken or turkey would be cooked. All methods provide a wonderful wild game meat. About 3 ounces of squirrel meat has 100 calories and 18 grams of protein. Any way you cook it, squirrel meat, prepared properly, will end up being an aromatic, flavorful, and wonderful tasting wild game experience.

BAKED SQUIRREL

SERVES 4

¼ cup white vinegar

4 tablespoons salt

4 squirrels (skinned, cleaned and de-boned; use hind legs and meaty back; cut into serving pieces)

1 teaspoon meat tenderizer

1 teaspoon black pepper

1–1½ cups all-purpose flour

Vegetable oil, as needed, for frying

2 tablespoons unsalted butter

1 yellow onion, peeled and chopped

1 green bell pepper, seeded and chopped

4 tablespoons red wine

1 can cream of mushroom soup

In a bowl, add the vinegar and salt, and whisk until salt has dissolved. Add the squirrel meat, and fill with water, enough to cover the squirrel. Let soak for 2 hours. Remove the meat and toss with the tenderizer and pepper. Next, roll in flour.

Preheat the oven to 350°F.

Add the oil to a large skillet over medium-high heat. When hot, add the squirrel and fry until golden-brown. Remove the meat from the skillet and transfer to a baking dish. Set aside.

Melt the butter in the skillet and add the onion and bell pepper. Sauté until vegetables are soft. Add the wine and cream of mushroom soup. Mix well, then pour over the squirrel in the baking dish. Bake in the oven for 30 minutes, or until squirrel is cooked through.

Adapted from the recipe by Cooks.com.

WINE SUGGESTION:

Porcupine Ridge Syrah

The wine is vivid purple on appearance, and the nose shows a classic abundance of violets and spice. Intense aromas of blackberries, black cherry, ripe plums, and brambles create an intriguing nose. The dark berry fruit of the nose follows through onto the mid-palate, with notes of black pepper, cloves, black cardamom, and sweet tobacco. The wine is balanced and focused, elegant yet juicy, with grippy tannins and integrated acidity. The wine lingers with hints of dried herbs, black olives, graphite, and tar.

BELGIAN SQUIRREL

SERVES 6

½ cup unsalted butter

3 large squirrels (skinned, cleaned and de-boned; use hind legs and meaty back; cut into serving pieces)

2 white onions, peeled and sliced

3 tablespoons white vinegar

⅛ teaspoon dried thyme

Salt and black pepper, to taste

18 pitted prunes

1½ teaspoons all-purpose flour

1 cup cold water

Preheat the oven to 375°F.

Melt the butter in a large skillet over medium heat. Add the squirrel pieces and fry until browned on all sides, but do not cook through. Remove the meat to a large Dutch oven or oven-safe crock. Set aside.

Add the onions to the butter in the skillet and cook, stirring occasionally, until tender and browned. Add the onions and butter into the pot with the squirrel. Fill the pot with enough water to almost cover the meat. Mix in the vinegar and season with thyme, salt, and pepper. Cover and place in the oven.

Bake for 45 minutes. Remove the pot and add the prunes. Return to the oven and reduce the heat to 325°F. Continue baking for another 45 minutes.

Remove the pot from the oven. Mix the flour and cold water together in a cup. Use a slotted spoon to remove the meat and prunes to a serving dish. Set the pot on the stove and bring to a boil over medium-high heat. Stir in the flour and water and simmer, stirring constantly, until a gravy forms and is thick enough to coat the back of a spoon. Serve the meat with the gravy.

Adapted from the recipe by AllRecipes.com.

WINE SUGGESTION:

Porcupine Ridge Merlot

The nose is intense and entices with its red currant, ripe dark plum, black cherry, and fruitcake aromas with whiffs of vanilla, baking spices, and incense. The palate shows more dark fruit with flavors of brambles, boysenberry, blackberry, and blueberry and a touch of violets. The wine is medium-bodied, smooth, and balanced with cocoa powdery tannins. Dark chocolate and hints of garrigue lingers on a classic finish. Drinks exceptionally well now or enjoy within the next two to three years with beef carpaccio, roast chicken or pork loin, cottage pie, lamb kofta, tomato-based pasta dishes, or this unique Belgian Squirrel dish.

SQUIRREL COUNTRY SAUSAGE

MAKES ABOUT 5 POUNDS

4½ pounds squirrel (about 15 squirrels; skinned, cleaned and de-boned; use hind legs and meaty back; cut into pieces)

2 pounds fresh seasoned pork sausage

3 teaspoons unsalted butter

1 white onion, peeled and minced

3 cloves garlic, peeled and minced

1 tablespoon fresh sage

2 teaspoons dried basil

1 tablespoon chili powder

4 tablespoons fresh Italian flat-leaf parsley

1 teaspoon dried thyme

2 tablespoon salt

1 tablespoon black pepper

Add the squirrel meat and pork sausage to a food processor and chop. Transfer to a bowl and set aside.

In a skillet over medium heat, melt the butter and then add the onion and garlic. Sauté until the onions are soft. Remove from heat and add to the bowl with the meat. Add the sage, basil, chili powder, parsley, thyme, salt, and pepper. Mix well to combine.

Note: To test the seasonings, form a small patty of the sausage mixture and fry in the skillet with a little melted butter. Taste and adjust seasonings accordingly.

Form the sausage mixture into small patties. Refrigerate or freeze until ready to use. Great on the grill or use with your favorite sausage recipes. Crumble for tasty pizza topping, too.

Adapted from the recipe by the Missouri Department of Conservation.

WINE SUGGESTION:

Porcupine Ridge Sauvignon Blanc

The nose is delicate and saline, but intrigues with its apple blossom, green melon, and stone fruit aromas and gentle whiffs of dill, lime, grapefruit, and nettles. The palate is smooth and textured and surprises with its intensity of green and tropical fruit flavors, showing nectarine, pear, papaya, greengage, even gooseberry. The wine is supple and round, yet focused, with balanced acidity. It finishes with white peach, green fig, and lemongrass lingering in the mouth with hints of tarragon and chalk—perfect for summer.

LARGE GAME

AMERICAN BISON

Bison bison

The American bison is often incorrectly referred to as a buffalo; bison are not true buffalo. The earliest bison (about 10,000 BC) roamed the great bison belt—a huge segment of prime grassland from Alaska to northern Mexico. By the early eighteenth century, bison populations exceeded 60 million animals! Unfortunately, they were decimated to near extinction by commercial hunting, and by the late 1800s, only 541 animals were said to remain. Today, there are about 30,000 bison mostly in the Rocky Mountain National Park systems and in smaller private bison herds raised for conservation and restoration efforts. Some of these herds are raised strictly for the sale of bison meat throughout North America.

There are two subspecies: the plains bison and the larger wood bison. In North America, bison are the heaviest land animals and the second tallest; only moose are taller. Male bison can weigh between 1,000 to 2,000 pounds and stand 5 to 6½ feet tall. They appear slow-moving but can reach speeds of 35 to 40 mph. Not impressed? Consider this: bison can also jump as high as 6 feet from a standing position!

It isn't wise to annoy a bison; they're *very* unpredictable and have *extremely* short fuses. It only takes one wrong move to provoke a bison into attack mode. Bison can gore, stomp, and crush any threat they perceive as potential danger, leaving man or beast in a heap of broken bones. (Now you know why we eat them.)

Bison, like elk and mule deer, are an iconic western species with a historic and colorful background in the American West. It can be hard to imagine hunting bison when 60 million of them roamed North America. Today, through conservation efforts mostly funded by hunters, Yellowstone has the largest huntable, free-ranging bison herd in North America. There are also huntable wild herds in Alaska, Arizona, Montana, South Dakota, Utah, Wyoming, the Crow Reservation in Montana, and in Canada. Wyoming, though, is a top choice to draw a bison tag.

Bison are bigger than Africa's notorious Cape buffalo. Literally, that's good food for thought. Choose a caliber that will penetrate their heavy hide, muscle, and bones. Bullet type and shot placement are also critical. A .30-06 with a heavy bullet is a *minimum* caliber. If a hunter can shoot heavier calibers comfortably and accurately, they would be better choices. Use only premium, controlled-expansion bullets to ensure deep penetration through a bison's thick hide, muscle, and bone. Avoid shots to the shoulder or hump. Instead, shoot at the lower third of the body so the bullet penetrates the lungs and/or heart. As with any massive, dangerous big game, always be prepared to make a quick follow-up shot.

For anyone who craves red meat, bison venison is firmly seated at the top of the flavor and tenderness category of all big game animals. Simply put, when field-dressed properly and prepared correctly in the kitchen, it is scrumptious. To risk using an overused phrase, bison is the original *grass-fed* critter. Bison meat is rich in flavor, low in fat, and high in protein. Its meat is a terrific substitute for beef and is said to be lower in calories and cholesterol than beef, pork, turkey, skinless chicken, and some fish. According the USDA, bison meat is also rich in iron, zinc, vitamin B12, omega 3-fatty acids, and the antioxidant selenium. Bison meat can't be compared to other big game venison like moose, elk, deer, caribou, etc. It is in a totally separate category when it comes to its taste, texture, and cooking methods. Bison meat can easily replace all beef recipes without any chance of being identified as a wild game meat. However, it should always be taken care of properly from field to table.

Bison Blue Cheeseburger

BISON BLUE CHEESEBURGER

SERVES 6

1½ pounds ground bison

2 tablespoons Dijon mustard

1 tablespoon shallot, peeled and
 sautéed until soft

1 tablespoon garlic, peeled,
 minced, and sautéed until soft

1 teaspoon Worcestershire
 sauce

Kosher salt and black pepper,
 to taste

6 teaspoons blue cheese,
 divided

2 red onions, peeled and sliced

2 teaspoons olive oil, divided

1 teaspoon balsamic vinegar

2 fennel bulbs, thinly sliced

Hamburger buns, toasted

In a large bowl, add the bison, mustard, shallot, garlic, Worcestershire sauce, salt, and pepper. Mix well by hand (do not overmix) and form 6 patties. Insert 1 teaspoon of blue cheese in the center of each patty. Set aside.

In a small bowl, place the onion slices and drizzle with 1 teaspoon of olive oil and balsamic vinegar.

In a small grill-proof pan, add the sliced fennel and remaining teaspoon of olive oil.

Heat an outdoor grill or barbecue on high. Prepare the grill by brushing with oil or using grill nonstick spray. Grill the burgers to order. While the burgers are cooking, add the seasoned onions to the grill.

Add the grill-proof pan and sauté the fennel while the burgers and onions are cooking. (Note: you can also sauté the fennel over an electric or gas burner.)

Remove the onions and fennel when tender, and toss together in the bowl the onions were in.

Remove the burgers, and place on toasted hamburger buns along with lettuce, and/or your favorite condiments. Top with the sautéed onions and fennel and serve.

Adapted from the recipe by the National Bison Association.

WINE SUGGESTION:

Chateau Ste. Michelle Cold Creek Vineyard Cabernet Sauvignon

Planted in the 1970s, Cold Creek is one of Washington state's oldest and most acclaimed vineyards. Character builds season after season in the growth rings of the old woody vines. Sun-drenched growing conditions with low rainfall result in small berries with full-bodied flavors. This Cabernet has broad-shouldered structure, concentrated fruit character, and deep color.

BISON & BABY BROWN MUSHROOM SOUP

MAKES 10–12 CUPS

2 tablespoons olive oil

1 large yellow onion, peeled and
    chopped

4 cloves garlic, peeled and finely
    chopped

2 whole fresh jalapeño peppers, seeds
    removed, finely chopped

1 teaspoon salt

1 teaspoon black pepper

1 teaspoon crushed red pepper flakes

2 pounds ground bison

2 pounds baby brown mushrooms,
    sliced

6 cups vegetable stock

6 cups cold water

8 ounces cream cheese

1 bunch kale, veins removed, chopped

1 bunch fresh Italian flat-leaf parsley,
    chopped

2 cups quinoa, prepared according to
    package directions

Chopped scallions, for garnish

Heat the olive oil in a large stock pot over medium heat. Add the onion, garlic, and jalapeño. Sauté while adding the salt, pepper, and red pepper flakes. Add the bison and mushrooms and continue to sauté until the meat is cooked through. Add the vegetable stock and water. Reduce heat to low and allow to simmer. Add the cream cheese and continue to simmer. Right before serving, stir in the kale and parsley.

To serve, add ½ cup of the cooked quinoa into each serving bowl. Add the soup and garnish with chopped scallions.

Adapted from the recipe by the National Bison Association.

WINE SUGGESTION:

Chateau Ste. Michelle Indian Wells Merlot

The Indian Wells Merlot offers ripe berry fruit aromas and jammy flavors. This is a full-bodied style of warm climate Merlot with a round, supple finish. Chateau Ste. Michelle added Wahluke Slope Syrah to enhance the mouthfeel and rich fruit character.

GRILLED BISON MEATBALLS AND ROASTED VEGETABLE SKEWERS

SERVES 4

1 pound ground bison

¼ cup crumbled crackers
(about 6 small squares)

¼ cup fresh chopped cilantro
(or Italian flat-leaf parsley)

1 egg white, beaten

3 ounces crumbled feta cheese

3 tablespoons chopped
Kalamata (or black) olives

¾ teaspoon ground cinnamon

¾ teaspoon salt

¾ teaspoon black pepper

2 cloves garlic, peeled and
finely minced

2 large yellow onions, peeled
and cut into wedges

3 multicolor bell peppers,
seeded and cut into 1½-inch
squares

2 medium zucchini, sliced into
⅜-inch rounds

Spicy Orange Barbecue Sauce,
recipe follows

Spicy Orange Barbecue Sauce

¼ cup orange marmalade

1 tablespoon chili powder

1 teaspoon dry mustard

1 teaspoon vinegar

In a medium bowl, add the bison, crackers, cilantro, egg white, feta cheese, olives, cinnamon, salt, black pepper, and garlic. Mix well until blended. Shape into 8 large meatballs.

To prepare the barbecue sauce, in a small bowl, add the marmalade, chili powder, dry mustard, and vinegar. Mix well until combined. Set aside.

Prepare 4 metal grilling skewers (note: if using wooden skewers, soak in water for at least 30 minutes before grilling) by alternating the bison meatballs (2 per skewer) with the onion wedges, bell pepper, and zucchini.

Heat an outdoor grill or barbecue on high. Prepare the grill by brushing with oil or using grill nonstick spray. Place the skewers on the grill for 5 minutes while basting with the Spicy Orange Barbecue Sauce. Turn the skewers over, baste, and continuing to grill. Skewers are ready when the vegetables are tender and slightly charred and the bison meatballs are cooked through. Remove from grill and serve immediately.

This recipe is adapted from a recipe by the National Bison Association.

WINE SUGGESTION:

Chateau Ste. Michelle Columbia Valley Cabernet Sauvignon

Chateau Ste. Michelle crafts their Columbia Valley Cabernet to highlight concentrated Washington state red fruit in an accessible style. This is an inviting Cab with plenty of complexity and structure with silky tannins. It's also very versatile with food. Enjoy it with beef or these Grilled Bison Meatballs.

AMERICAN BLACK BEAR

Ursus americanus

The habitat of the American black bear spans throughout most of North America—from Alaska to northern Mexico. Black bears, and their sixteen subspecies, are the smallest of the North American bear species (Polar, brown, and grizzly bears). Not all black bears have black fur. The hide colors range from totally black, to black with a white patch, light brown, gray, cinnamon, very dark brown to even pure white (which is found only on the island archipelago of southern British Columbia). Black, however, is the bear's predominant color.

Black bears prefer conifer and deciduous forests with thick understories. Their variable diet, however, allows them to adapt to a variety of habitats. Because they are omnivorous, bears eat a wide selection of foods including acorns and other nuts, fruits, honey, berries, roots, fish, insects, larvae, grass, and carrion. When the opportunity arises, they will hunt and eat adult and fawn deer, elk, moose, caribou, and livestock.

An adult black bear is about 3 feet tall at the shoulder and 6½ feet long. Adult males are considerably larger than adult females. A large male can exceed 600 pounds, while females seldom reach 250 pounds. The largest black bear on record was a male boar taken by a hunter in New Brunswick, Canada, in 1972. This trophy bear field dressed at an amazing 902 pounds and had an estimated live weight of 1,000 pounds. The bear measured 7 feet 9 inches long.

Other than whitetails, black bears are the most pursued big game animal in North America. The black bear's imposing size, elusiveness, honed senses, and potential ferocity make it a challenging game animal. The Canadian provinces have the largest density of black bears and, therefore, offer a high success rate for hunters. There is also excellent black bear hunting throughout the United States. The best places to hunt black bear are in Arizona, with Montana, Alaska, Pennsylvania, Colorado, Wisconsin, Idaho, and California all running close behind. These states offer plenty of non-resident tags (with some states offering both spring and summer seasons).

Bear hunting methods include spot-and-stalk, trailing with dogs, using predator calls, posting, and bait site hunting—where legal. Hunters must pay meticulous attention to wind direction, as black bears have an exceptionally sharp sense of smell. Their keen ears are stereophonic. A hunter may fool a bear's sight, but the bear's other senses can easily help it avoid a hunter.

Some hunters are squeamish about eating black bear; but trust this, the meat is delectable if it is handled and prepared properly from field to table. Bear meat will become rank and tough when handled incorrectly after the kill. The taste of black bear meat is said to be similar to venison, only sweeter. Like venison, it's a deeper red meat than beef, with a texture similar to pork. In the spring, bear come out of hibernation with much less fat; so, the flavor and tenderness of spring bear is better than fall bear. A younger bear is expectedly more tender than an old bear.

An average black bear will provide about 90 or more pounds of boneless meat. Bear venison is an excellent source of riboflavin, iron, protein, thiamin, niacin, and phosphorus. It is recommended to cut away as much fat as possible from bear meat as soon as it is killed. There will still be plenty of marbling throughout the meat to flavor most cuts. Also, leaving fat on the bear is said to increase the likelihood of the meat becoming rancid later in the processing. Use proper cooking techniques to help ensure bear meat is safe to eat.

SAFELY COOKING BEAR MEAT

According to the CDC, black bear meat can be a carrier of *Trichinella spiralis* and *Toxoplasma gondii*, the parasites that cause the diseases trichinosis and toxoplasmosis in humans. Proper cooking techniques can ensure that your bear meat is safe to eat. Like pork, the proper cooking temperature for bear meat is 375°F for 20 to 25 minutes per pound. Internal cooking temperature should reach 160°F for 3 minutes or more before consumption. Cook until there is no trace of pink meat or fluid, paying close attention to areas around the joints and close to the bone. Freezing meat does not always kill these parasites. Connoisseurs of bear meat suggest freezing, canning, or eating the meat within one week of the kill, as the flavor becomes stronger with age. Trim fat from the meat especially well and, as with all meat, good wrapping and sealing is recommended.

GRILLED SPICED BLACK BEAR TENDERLOIN

SERVES 2

1 teaspoon salt

1½ teaspoons black pepper

1½ teaspoons ground allspice

¾ teaspoon ground cinnamon

¾ teaspoon ground clove

½ teaspoon ground nutmeg

1 tablespoon olive oil

1 pound bear tenderloin or backstrap, trimmed of all fat and silver skin

In a small bowl, add the salt, pepper, allspice, cinnamon, clove, and nutmeg. Drizzle the olive oil while stirring until a paste is formed.

Rub all sides of the trimmed tenderloin evenly with the spice mixture and set aside.

Heat an outdoor grill or barbecue to medium heat. Prepare the grill by brushing with oil or using grill nonstick spray. Grill the bear steaks until fully cooked, turning occasionally (note: watch for flareups from any dripping fat; the more fat trimmed off prior to grilling, the better). Bear meat should reach an internal temperature of 160°F before consuming.

Adapted from the recipe by the New Jersey Division of Fish & Wildlife.

WINE SUGGESTION:

Chateau Ste. Michelle Columbia Valley Dry Riesling

The Chateau Ste. Michelle Dry Riesling is a dry, refreshing style of Riesling with beautiful fruit flavors, crisp acidity, and an elegant finish. It offers inviting sweet citrus aromas and flavors. This is an incredibly versatile food wine.

BLACK BEAR MEATLOAF

SERVES 4

3 pounds ground bear meat

1 pound ground beef (with high fat content)

3 eggs, beaten

1½ cups breadcrumbs

1 can (8 ounces) mushrooms

¼ cup ketchup

Garlic powder, to taste

Black pepper, to taste

3 cans Campbell's French Onion Soup, divided

Preheat the oven to 350°F.

In a large bowl, add the ground bear meat, ground beef, eggs, breadcrumbs, mushrooms, ketchup, garlic powder, and pepper. Strain the liquid from two of the cans of the French Onion Soup and reserve. Add the onions from the two cans to the meat mixture. Mix well with hands, but do not overmix.

Form the meat mixture into a loaf and carefully set on a roasting pan. Pour the liquid from the two cans slowly over the top of the loaf, along with the whole third can of the soup.

Place the pan in the oven and bake for 2½ hours, or until done. Bear meat should reach an internal temperature of 160°F before consuming.

Adapted from the recipe by the New Jersey Division of Fish & Wildlife.

WINE SUGGESTION:

Chateau Ste. Michelle Columbia Valley Syrah

The Columbia Valley Syrah is a soft, jammy Syrah made in an approachable and fruit-forward style. This is an enjoyable, easy-to-drink red.

CHARCOAL-GRILLED BEAR RIBS

SERVES 2–4

1 full or half rack of ribs, trimmed of all fat, gristle, and silver skin. If ribs are too long, saw in half

Dry Spice Rub
¼ cup brown sugar
2 teaspoons kosher salt
2 teaspoons black pepper
2 teaspoons smoked paprika
1 teaspoon garlic powder
1 teaspoon onion powder
1 teaspoon ground mustard
½ teaspoon cinnamon
½ teaspoon celery salt
¼ teaspoon cayenne pepper

For the spice rub, in a small bowl, add the brown sugar, salt, pepper, paprika, garlic powder, onion powder, ground mustard, cinnamon, celery salt, and cayenne pepper. Use a fork to crush any lumps. Store in an airtight container for up to one month.

Prepare the ribs by rubbing all sides of the rib racks liberally with the Dry Spice Rub.

Prepare an outdoor charcoal barbecue for low, indirect heat. Add smoke wood chunks to the charcoal to create a fragrant smoke on the meat. To prevent charring, monitor the temperature with a grilling thermometer.

Place the ribs on the grill and cook slowly for 6 to 10 hours, or until desired doneness, turning occasionally and re-seasoning. Bear meat should reach an internal temperature of 160°F before consuming.

Adapted from the recipe by the New Jersey Division of Fish & Wildlife.

WINE SUGGESTION:

Chateau Ste. Michelle Columbia Valley Merlot

Chateau Ste. Michelle crafts this wine to be their complex yet approachable Merlot. The wine offers aromas of black cherry, leather, and spice with layers of rich, dark red fruit flavors and a long, smooth, sweet finish. A touch of Syrah adds a jammy fruit character. Think of this wine as a great "everyday red."

CARIBOU (REINDEER)

Rangifer tarandus

Caribou (a.k.a. reindeer) are the third largest members within the family of deer (*Cervidae*). Only moose and elk are larger. Caribou are broadly classified into three different subspecies: Barren Ground Caribou (*Rangifer articus articus*), Woodland Caribou (*Rangifer caribou caribou*), and Mountain Caribou (*Rangifer montanus*). Within the continental United States, small herds of caribou inhabit Idaho, Montana, and Minnesota. In Alaska, large populations of herds of caribou are dispersed throughout the state. Alaska has predominantly the Barren ground caribou. Canada harbors caribou in several of the country's provinces. The Canadian province of Newfoundland is the only place in the world where woodland caribou can be hunted.

Caribou have evolved large, concave hoofs that splay widely apart to support them in both snow and soft tundra. Splayed hooves are also effective paddles for swimming—and caribou do a lot of swimming. Both sexes of caribou grow antlers. Adult bulls have large and massive antlers, and adult cows have smaller spindly and shorter antlers. An adult bull can weigh, on average, 350 to 400 pounds (yet weights of 700 pounds are possible). Mature females average 175 to 225 pounds. Caribou herds in northern and southwestern Alaska winter in the boreal forest, but other times of the year, they prefer treeless tundra and mountains where they escape from the relentless hordes of mosquitos.

Caribou must continually keep moving (migrating) to locate ample food. Large caribou herds most often migrate extreme distances (up to 400 miles or more) between summer and winter ranges. Smaller herds may not migrate at all. In summer (May to late August), caribou eat the leaves of willows, sedges, flowering tundra plants, and mushrooms. In September, caribou begin to forage on lichens (a.k.a. reindeer moss), dried sedges (a.k.a. grasslike plants), and small shrubs (mostly blueberry).

Cows and calves make guttural huffing sounds and are most vocal during calving and early summer. The vocalizations are primarily used as contact calls. Bulls only vocalize during the rut or breeding season. Bull vocalizations are surprisingly less guttural than cows and calves.

It is best to hunt caribou with a licensed, experienced outfitter or guide that uses horses, Argos, or bush planes to access caribou country. The most important part of the hunt is to locate caribou herds from high points. After that, walking and stalking is the primary tactic. To locate caribou, quality optics are a must-have including a spotting scope, binoculars, and rifle scope. Top rifle calibers and bullet grain choices include .270/130 gr., .270 WSM/150 gr, .264 Win Mag 140 gr., .280

150 gr., .308 Win. 150 gr., and .30-06 180 gr. One accurate shot minimizes the amount of potential blood-shot meat.

Simply stated, caribou meat is enormously delicious. Just as beef and pork have different flavors, so does caribou meat. It has a specific taste unlike other species of deer meat. Many find caribou meat to be sweeter and more tender with a supple texture. Like other big game meats, caribou venison is a rich source of protein, has a high amount of B-vitamin and iron, and has a low fat content. It is vital to know, though, that timing plays a huge role in the texture and flavor of caribou meat. Caribou bulls killed during the rut tend to have tough meat. More importantly, the meat from a bull in rut has a *very* potent odor. While cooking it, many hunters end up not eating it because of the foul odor. Other than the rut, however, caribou venison is an excellent table fare and a prized game meat.

>>>

WINE SUGGESTION:

2016 DeLille Cellars Grand Ciel Syrah

Initially vibrant, rich, and fruit forward in the glass, the 2016 Syrah from Grand Ciel Vineyard gradually unveils smoke, grilled meat, and lavender blossom with a hint of tangerine pith. This incredibly savory and inviting nose is supported on the palate with generous blackberry and tapenade flavors and demonstrates marvelous balance throughout. Building in intensity with subsequent tastes, this wine nevertheless retains its tension and should age beautifully.

EASY BBQ REINDEER RIBS

MAKES 4 RACKS OF RIBS

2 racks of reindeer ribs
   (4–6 pounds total), cut in half
¾ cup brown sugar (or honey)
1 teaspoon smoked salt
   (or liquid smoke + salt)
1 tablespoon garlic powder
1 tablespoon paprika
¼ teaspoon ground cloves
⅛ teaspoon cinnamon
½ teaspoon chili powder
½ teaspoon ground cumin
Salt and black pepper, as
   needed

Barbecue Sauce
¾ cup ketchup
1 tablespoon white wine vinegar
2 teaspoons smoked paprika
2 tablespoons brown sugar
1 tablespoon Worcestershire
   sauce

Preheat the oven to 300°F.

Remove the tough membrane on the bone side of the ribs. This must be done for the most tender ribs. The membrane should peel off with a bit of pulling and elbow grease.

In a bowl, make the rub by adding the brown sugar, smoked salt, garlic powder, paprika, ground cloves, cinnamon, chili powder, and ground cumin. Mix well to combine.

Using your hands, apply the rub all over both sides of the ribs, using generous amounts. Then sprinkle the racks on both sides with salt and pepper.

Cut each of the two large racks in half and place all four meat-side down, on two sheets of aluminum foil (shiny side out). Covering the ribs will seal in the juices.

Lay rib packages on a baking sheet meat side down and bake for 2½ hours, or until the meat is tender and falls off the bone.

In a small bowl, make the Barbecue Sauce. Add the ketchup, vinegar, smoked paprika, brown sugar, and Worcestershire sauce. Whisk until well combined. Refrigerate until ready to use.

Remove from oven and let the ribs rest for 10 minutes while you preheat an outdoor grill on high. Remove the foil and grill ribs for 4 to 5 minutes on each side while basting with the barbecue sauce. Remove and serve.

Adapted from the recipe by Sonya Andreanoff, Alaskan Foodie.

REINDEER STROGANOFF

SERVES 4–6

1½ pounds reindeer steak or
  boneless stewing meat
½ cup all-purpose flour, divided
½ teaspoon salt
3 tablespoons bacon fat
1 clove garlic, peeled and
  minced
2 small yellow onions, peeled
  and chopped
½ pound wild mushrooms,
  chopped
1 tablespoon Worcestershire
  sauce
1 beef bouillon cube, dissolved
  in 1 cup hot water
1 cup sour cream
Steamed rice or noodles, as
  needed
Paprika, as needed, for garnish

Use a kitchen mallet to pound the reindeer steak or stew meat to tenderize. Then cut into ½-inch strips. Dredge the strips in ¼ cup flour and salt. Set aside.

In a large cast-iron skillet or Dutch oven over medium-high heat, add the bacon fat. When hot, add the garlic, onions, and mushrooms. Sauté for 5 minutes, then remove and set aside. Add the reindeer strips to the pot and cook on all sides until brown. Remove the strips from the pan and set aside. Add the remaining ¼ cup flour to the pot, along with the Worcestershire and the bouillon. Reduce heat to low and cook until thickened, then add the sour cream. Continue to cook on low heat until gravy just barely simmers. Return the cooked meat and vegetables to the pot and simmer until the strips and vegetables are heated through. Serve over rice or noodles, and garnish with a sprinkle of paprika.

Adapted from the recipe by Sonya Andreanoff, Alaskan Foodie.

WINE SUGGESTION:

2017 DeLille Cellars Métier

This vintage presents a nose full of exceptional garigue aromas: wild rosemary, thyme, and lavender, with floral notes of wild berries and light wood smoke. Initially very tightly wound on the palate, with delicate juniper and strawberry leaf flavors, the wine is carried well by medium weight acidity and pleasantly grippy tannin. With time and air, the wine unfolds brilliantly, presenting pleasantly refreshing fruit flavors of plum, wild blackberries, and fig.

REINDEER STUFFED PEPPERS

SERVES 6

1 to 1½ pounds ground reindeer meat

2 tablespoons chopped yellow onion

2 tablespoons chopped celery

1 clove garlic, peeled and minced

1 package taco seasoning (or homemade equivalent)

1 (6-ounce) can tomato paste

1 cup water (or more)

⅛ teaspoon black pepper

⅛ teaspoon red pepper flakes

3 red bell peppers, halved, cored, and seeded

8 ounces shredded cheddar cheese, divided

Sour cream and salsa, as needed, optional

Preheat the oven to 350°F.

In a large skillet over medium heat, add the ground reindeer, onion, celery, and garlic. Brown the meat, stirring often, until the meat is well caramelized and the vegetables are soft. Drain the fat, if any, then add the taco seasoning, tomato paste, and water; adding more water if needed to make it saucy. Add the black pepper and red pepper flakes while continuing to stir. Cook until the meat mixture is thick but still saucy (about 10 minutes).

Meanwhile, parboil the peppers in a little boiling water for 3 minutes each, then drain. Place the peppers in a baking dish. Stir half of the cheese into the reindeer mixture and then fill the peppers with the meat mixture. Top each pepper with the remaining cheese. Place in the oven and bake for 15 to 20 minutes, or until hot and bubbly and the peppers are tender. Serve with sour cream and salsa, if desired.

Adapted from the recipe by Sonya Andreanoff, Alaskan Foodie.

WINE SUGGESTION:

2017 DeLille Cellars D2

The D2 offers abundant dried cranberry and raspberry aromas surging from the glass, with intertwined darker fruit notes of cassis, blueberry, and blackberry. Delicately balanced oak influence contributes cocoa and coffee bean notes while remaining completely respectful of the fruit. This appealing wine is vibrant and extraordinarily fresh on the palate, with persistent fruit flavors of pomegranate and blueberry. Understated and subtle tannin provides welcome structure, while excellent early integration offers accessibility, generosity, and abundant pleasure despite the wine's youth.

ELK

Cervus

Elk (a.k.a. Wapiti) are the second largest members within the family of deer (*Cervidae*). Only moose are larger. There are four subspecies of elk in North America; the largest bodied elk is the Roosevelt (a.k.a. Olympic), closely followed by the Rocky Mountain (a.k.a. American), then the Manitoban, and the smallest is the Tule elk.

A few eastern states offer limited quotas for hunting Rocky Mountain elk. However, elk are most often found in many western states, particularly in the Rocky Mountains. Colorado has the largest population of Rocky Mountain Elk with about 300,000 animals, making it a top-notch state to take an elk. Roosevelt elk are found in the temperate forests of Washington, Oregon, northern California, and in Canada's British Columbia. Tule elk are found only in central California.

Along with bison (a.k.a. buffalo), elk were a primary food source of Native Americans. Today, other than white-tailed deer, elk are the second most popular hunted big game animal.

While deer are primarily browsers, elk are mainly grazers (akin to cattle), but they also browse. Their diet varies throughout the seasons. During spring and summer, elk graze on grasses, sedges, berries, and a wide variety of flowering plants. As fall approaches, elk switch to browsing an assorted variety of buds, sprouts, tips of branches, bark, leaves, brush, and will continue to graze on grasses that are not snow covered. Elk generally eat 8 to 15 pounds of vegetation per day. In winter, elk migrate to lower elevations to find food. Tule elk have little need to migrate from their native terrain, as their food sources remain available throughout the seasons.

Many hunters who pursue large-antlered game, including moose, elk, and caribou, say wapiti provide a more challenging hunt. An elk hunter has to have more diverse skills, including tracking, calling, spot and stalking, and a deeper understanding of elk behaviors and habits. Many old-time elk hunters claim wapiti can be as cunning as an old savvy whitetail buck.

Part of the allure of elk hunting is that elk bulls are very vocal—making bugles, barks, chuckles, and glunking sounds. Elk cows make mews, whines, and barks. Knowing how to realistically mimic elk sounds will make all the difference in whether a hunter will be eating *pasta e fagiole* or elk steak for the rest of the year.

First and foremost, time your elk hunt to the rut, which usually takes place the last few weeks in September and occasionally runs into the first week of October. Rut hunting helps hunters locate bulls much more effectively. Outside of the rut, finding a good bull elk can be difficult. On DIY elk hunts, savvy hunters need to know the area as well as possible. Use topographical maps to become familiar with elevations, terrain, etc. Glassing elk in open areas can account for *some* sightings, most of which, however, will be cows and young bulls. Instead, concentrate glassing in the thickest cover that can be found. Hunt the edges of mesas (high flat areas) and along ridgetops, stopping often to glass any ravines, gullies, gorges, and valleys below. Move along the middle of a mesa slowly and carefully, stopping every 100 yards to carefully glass ahead. Pay particular attention to thick stands of standing firs and *blowdowns*. Many trophy bull elk have been killed as they got up from thick tangles of blowdowns. Research shows most elk are taken in the afternoons (2 p.m. to when legal light ends), rather than other times of the day, including dawn.

Elk meat has been an important staple ever since our earliest ancestors pursued game. Native American Indians hunted elk more often than they did the migrating herds of buffalo. Elk also provided the hordes of pioneer settlers with a reliable source of red meat. If 100 hunters were asked what wild game meat they prized most, an overwhelming consensus would undoubtedly be elk. And, why not? Elk venison is a delectable red meat that is high in protein and low in fat. Most hunters claim the taste of elk meat is "indistinguishable" from beef. Others say elk meat is "sweeter" than beef.

Elk Burgers

ELK BURGERS

SERVES 6

1½–2 pounds ground elk
Garlic salt, as needed, to taste
1 tablespoon olive oil, or as
 needed
6 ciabatta buns

In a bowl, add the elk and season to desired taste with garlic salt. Because elk is very lean, the ground meat will stick together with the addition of a splash of olive oil. To savor the taste of grilled elk meat, do not add additional seasonings.

Heat an outdoor grill or barbecue to medium-high heat. Prepare the grill by brushing with oil or using grill nonstick spray. Grill the elk burgers, turning occasionally, until medium rare (about 6 to 8 minutes).

Serve the elk burgers on toasted ciabatta buns with your favorite toppings and condiments.

Adapted from the recipe by Northfork Bison.

WINE SUGGESTION:

Chateau Ste. Michelle Indian Wells Red Blend

The Indian Wells Red Blend is an easy to enjoy red from warmer climate vineyards. The wine reflects the rich, round powerful style of Washington fruit, highlighting nine varietals. It is a true example of the art of blending. The wine offers jammy boysenberry flavors from the Syrah with a luscious concentration from the Merlot. This is a great match with the Elk Burgers.

ROASTED ELK IN BEER SAUCE

SERVES 4

1 elk roast (about 3 to 4 pounds)

1 yellow onion, peeled and
  sliced

½ cup chili sauce

2 tablespoons brown sugar

2 cloves garlic, peeled and
  minced

12 ounces beer

Salt and black pepper, to taste

Preheat the oven to 350°F.

Place the elk roast in a 9 x 13 baking dish. Cover with the sliced onions.

In a bowl, add the chili sauce, brown sugar, garlic, beer, salt, and pepper. Mix until well combined. Slowly pour over the onions and roast in the pan.

Cover the dish with aluminum foil and roast for 3½ to 4 hours or until elk is cooked through.

Adapted from the recipe by Northfork Bison.

WINE SUGGESTION:

Chateau Ste. Michelle Canoe Ridge Estate Merlot

Chateau Ste. Michelle's Canoe Ridge Estate Merlot consistently exhibits elegance, concentration, and fine tannins. This Merlot exhibits dark cherry fruit with an opulent mouthfeel and structure. Enjoy this wine with the Roasted Elk in Beer Sauce.

ELK MEDALLIONS WITH CRANBERRY SAUCE

SERVES 4

1 cup light white wine

1 shallot, peeled and chopped

4 elk medallions

1 sprig fresh thyme

Salt and black pepper, to taste

1 tablespoon unsalted butter, as needed

1 tablespoon vegetable oil, as needed

Cranberry Sauce

1 cup beef stock

¼ cup dried cranberries

¼ cup heavy cream

Salt and black pepper, to taste

In a bowl, add the wine and shallots. Stir well and add the elk medallions, thyme, and salt and black pepper. Allow to marinate for 2 hours. Remove the medallions, reserving the marinade. Dry the medallions with paper towels and set aside.

Heat a large skillet over medium-high heat. Combine the butter and oil and add to the pan. When hot, add the medallions. Cook 3 to 5 minutes per side. Remove from the pan, set aside, and cover.

To make the Cranberry Sauce, pour the reserved marinade into the skillet, and heat on high. Add the beef stock and cranberries. Reduce the liquid by half. Add the cream and bring the sauce to the desired consistency and adjust the seasoning with salt and pepper, as needed.

Transfer the elk medallions to a serving platter and serve with the Cranberry Sauce.

Adapted from the recipe by Northfork Bison.

WINE SUGGESTION:

Chateau Ste. Michelle & Dr. Loosen Eroica Riesling

Eroica Riesling offers sweet lime and mandarin orange aromas with subtle mineral notes. The mouth-watering acidity is beautifully balanced by flavorful Washington Riesling fruit. Eroica is a blended statement of the finest Riesling vineyards in the state. To achieve their Eroica style, Chateau Ste. Michelle strives for bright fruit with crisp acidity and enhanced minerality.

MOOSE

Alces alces

Ice age rock art on a fjord at the mouth of the Barents Sea is covered with drawings depicting herds of moose and reindeer. These carvings document how mankind hunted *Megaloceros giganteus* since stone-age humans hurled their first spears. This mega deer was a true gargantuan that roamed our planet about 400,000 years ago and only died out about 7,000 years ago. Standing eight feet tall at the shoulder, it had antlers that were 11 feet wide or more! Modern moose are not nearly as impressive but are still the largest deer within the *Cervidae* family (moose, elk, caribou, mule deer, and white-tailed deer) and their body and antler sizes, even today, are quite imposing.

Moose are hunted throughout Eurasia, North America, and Scandinavia. Most *sport* hunting for moose is done in United States and Canada. There are four subspecies of moose in North America: the Alaskan-Yukon (the largest), the Eastern and Western, and the Shiras moose (the smallest). An Alaskan-Yukon bull can weigh 1,400 pounds and stand 7 feet tall. A Shiras bull generally weighs about 700 to 800 pounds and barely stands 6 feet tall.

All four subspecies of moose inhabit a variety of terrains, including boreal and mixed deciduous forests, mountains, clear-cuts, logged-over woodlands, and burned-out areas. These are places where moose find grasses, fireweed, birch, willow, alder, moss, lichen, pinecones, leaves, bark, twigs, buds, and shrubs. Many of these terrain areas also provide moose protection from predators and severe weather.

All subspecies of moose can be hunted using several important tactics to help put meat in the freezer and antlers on the wall. Moose are most often found inhabiting areas close to water (ponds, lakes, rivers, marshes, or bogs) where they feed on a variety of succulent aquatic plants like water lilies. Hunters can also find bulls seeking estrus cows in open marshes, bogs, logged-over areas, and clear-cuts where they can call or rake an antler to attract both bulls and cows.

Moose are most vocal during the rut (September and early October) and eagerly respond to calling tactics including cow mews and bull grunts. When a cow is located, especially during the rut, have patience to see if a bull shows up. If the cow is making long, mewing vocalizations, it is almost a guarantee she will attract a bull. Sometimes, it takes an hour or more for the bull to appear; other times, he comes into view in minutes.

Savvy moose hunters generally concentrate their efforts to one specific area in the morning and another in the evening. During the late morning, set up on a high point and glass lowlands to locate moose. During the midday, hunt for moose in wooded areas where cows like to rest. Like all deer, moose are most active from dusk to dawn.

Some adventurous hunters pursue moose while floating quietly along waterways. They must always be on the ready, as bulls are often spotted stepping from cover to an open shoreline. Additionally, still-hunting along shorelines of lakes, rivers, or ponds is an excellent tactic for hunting moose.

No matter where moose are stalked, hunters place an extremely high value on their meat. Properly cared for from field to table, moose meat is by far the most flavorful and scrumptious wild big-game meat. Moose venison can be as mouthwatering as any cut of tender beef or even veal. Note, I did not say it tastes like chicken, veal, or beef. The protein levels of moose meat are similar to that of beef, elk, and white-tailed deer. Like other wild harvested deer meats (elk, caribou, white-tailed deer, and mule deer) moose venison also has a low-fat content. Unlike some of the other four deer species, however, moose meat has a higher quantity of polyunsaturated fats. This makes its meat more flavorful than the venison with more saturated fats commonly found in the other four deer species. Remember, one well-placed shot reduces the amount of blood-shot meat that may have to be discarded and maximizes the delicious table fare to follow.

Moose Shepherd's Pie

MOOSE SHEPHERD'S PIE

SERVES 4–6

1½ pounds (2 large) russet potatoes, peeled and cubed

5 cloves garlic, peeled

2 large carrots, cut into bite-sized pieces

½ head cauliflower, chopped

1 slice bacon (for fat content)

1 pound ground moose mince (thawed or fresh)

2 tablespoons all-purpose flour

1 (11-ounce) can corn niblets, drained

1 cup beef broth

½ teaspoon salt

½ cup of salted butter

1 cup grated cheddar cheese, divided

½ cup almond milk

Fill two pots with water. Add the potatoes and garlic to one pot and boil until tender (about 15 minutes). In the other pot, boil the carrots. When carrots are almost tender, add the cauliflower to the pot. Cooking times for both pots should be about the same.

In a large cast-iron skillet over medium heat, fry the bacon until crisp. Remove from skillet and discard (or eat). Add the ground moose mince to the skillet with the bacon fat. Brown the meat on all sides. Sprinkle in the flour and add the drained corn, cooked carrots, and cauliflower. Stir in the beef broth and season with the salt. Reduce heat to low and let simmer until thickened.

While the skillet is simmering, drain the potatoes and add them to a bowl with the butter, ¾ cup of the cheese, and the almond milk. Mash with a potato masher.

Once the meat mixture has thickened (add more flour if necessary), flatten out the mixture with a spatula until smooth. Add the mashed potatoes on top of the meat mixture, smoothing out with the spatula. Sprinkle the remaining ¼ cup cheese over the top. Bake in the oven until the top is brown and the cheese is bubbly. Internal temperature should be at least 165°F.

Adapted from the recipe by All-About-Moose.com.

WINE SUGGESTION:

Grgich Hills Estate Merlot, Napa Valley

This robust Merlot will delight Cabernet Sauvignon lovers. On the nose, this Merlot offers layers of fruit—blueberry, raspberry, and cherry. The palate is elegantly structured with mouth-watering tannins and sprightly, well-balanced acidity. The fruit-forward berries on the nose reemerge on the palate with savory undertones of basil and rosemary. This harmonious wine displays a lasting and memorable finish. Pair it with grilled or roasted moose, game burgers, or venison.

MOOSE HAMBURGER SANDWICHES WITH DANISH FONTINA CHEESE

SERVES 4

4 slices thick-sliced bacon

Wild mushrooms, as needed, sliced

1 white onion, peeled and sliced

1 pound ground moose mince (¼ pound per patty)

Sundried tomatoes, as needed

4 slices Danish fontina cheese

4 ciabatta rolls, sliced and toasted

1 fresh tomato, sliced

Salt and black pepper, to taste

In a skillet over medium heat, fry the bacon until desired doneness. Remove the bacon and reserve. Add the mushrooms and onions, and sauté until tender. Remove and reserve.

Heat an outdoor grill or barbecue on high. Prepare the grill by brushing with oil or using grill nonstick spray. Grill the burgers to desired doneness, topping them with sundried tomatoes and a slice of cheese.

Remove the burgers, and place on toasted ciabatta buns along with sliced tomato, the sautéed onions and mushrooms, and bacon. Sprinkle the burgers with salt and pepper, and serve with your favorite condiments, such as mayonnaise and mustard.

Adapted from the recipe by All-About-Moose.com.

WINE SUGGESTION:

Grgich Hills Estate Zinfandel, Napa Valley

Grgich's rich and full-bodied Zinfandel is graced with an elegant structure and richly nuanced flavors of blackberries and ripe cherries. A subtle waft of roasted coffee beans and lightly toasted almonds entwines with soft raspberries in a luxuriously long and persistent finish. This food-friendly wine pairs beautifully with a wide array of dishes, such as sausage pizza, grilled shish-kabobs, or these moose burgers.

DUTCH OVEN MOOSE ROAST

SERVES 6

2 tablespoons coconut oil (or oil of preference)

1 sirloin tip moose roast (about 2¾ pounds)

1 medium yellow onion, peeled and chopped

4 cloves garlic, peeled and crushed

4 slices bacon

1 cup beef stock

½ cup red wine

2 carrots, peeled and chopped

2 celery stalks, chopped

Salt and black pepper, to taste

1 tablespoon fresh Italian flat-leaf parsley, chopped

1 fresh rosemary sprig

3–4 fresh sage leaves

3–4 fresh thyme sprigs

Preheat the oven to 250°F.

Place the Dutch oven over medium-high heat. Add the oil. When hot, add the moose roast and brown on all sides. Remove roast and set aside.

Lower the heat to low and add the onion to the pot. Simmer until onions are soft. Return the roast to the pot. Spoon some of the onions on top of the roast along with the crushed garlic. Lay the bacon strips on top of the roast. While the roast continues to simmer, add the beef stock and wine. Place the carrots and celery around the roast. Sprinkle the roast with salt and pepper, and arrange the parsley, rosemary, sage, and thyme on top and around the roast. Cover with a lid and let simmer another 15 minutes.

Transfer the Dutch oven to the oven and cook until roast is fully cooked and tender, about 6 hours, at an internal temperature of at least 145°F.

Adapted from the recipe by All-About-Moose.com.

WINE SUGGESTION:

Grgich Hills Estate Miljenko's Old Vine Zinfandel

This full-bodied, aromatic Zinfandel is lavished with aromas of enticing plums, warm sandalwood, and white pepper. The wine's concentrated flavors and smooth tannins make it the perfect partner for savory duck and game meats.

MOUNTAIN LION

Puma concolor

The American Mountain lion is known by more than eighty names, one of which is "the cat with many names." Creative, huh? The most commonly used names include mountain lion, cougar, puma, panther, catamount, and painter. No matter what you call the charismatic cougar, it's still the same cat—the mountain lion—the largest of the small cat species.

Cougars used to be *extremely* secretive animals. In the past, they were rarely seen by anyone enjoying the outdoors. That is not the case any longer. Because they are protected in many states, their population numbers have increased. They have become more habitualized to humans, making sightings more frequent. Unfortunately, lion attacks (some fatal), on hikers, campers, hunters, and even cyclists have increased considerably in recent years.

Mountain lions once inhabited every state in the country. Nowadays, they mostly reside in sixteen states (Washington, Oregon, California, Nevada, Arizona, Utah, Idaho, Montana, Wyoming, Colorado, Nebraska, New Mexico, South Dakota, North Dakota, Texas, and a small endangered population in Florida).

Cougars prefer locations with dense undergrowth. They are also found in deserts, humid coast forests, arid hillsides, scrub and oak woodlands, and can live from sea level to snow-covered mountain peaks. Cougars usually live about ten years in the wild. In states where they are hunted, their general lifespan is five to seven years. Mountain lions usually have territories of about 100 square miles, but their territory can be considerably expanded during mating season.

Mother Nature perfectly designed the mountain lion's body for one purpose: the kill. Adult lions can measure 8 feet long from nose to tail and weigh 200 pounds. They have an 80 percent success kill rate and can take down prey five times their own size. Lions stalk prey silently, and when they're ready to pounce, their powerful muscles propel them in short bursts of speeds up to 50 mph. This amazing kittycat is also capable of leaping 18 feet straight up in the air. Interestingly, unlike the cats of the *Panthera* family (including lions, leopards, tigers, and jaguars, which are all capable of roaring), mountain lions can't roar. They are part of the *Feline* family and, like cheetahs, they mostly purr, but they also snarl, growl, and make moaning groans.

Hunting for mountain lions is predominantly done with a guide and a pack of hounds. It is possible, though, to hunt lions using other tactics. When it comes to stalking cougars, start with identifying signs left by lions. Lions leave scat that is not segmented and contains animal hair. Cougars are opportunistic feeders, and they will eat almost any animal—big or small—that crosses their path.

They will even kill and eat other lions! Fresh lion tracks show four toes, a bi-lobed frontal heel pad and tri-lobed pad at the rear. An adult lion track usually measures 3 to 4 inches long.

Like a lot of predators, lions can be lured in using calls. The sound of a deer in distress, a rabbit squealing, and even the sound of a female cougar in estrus can attract another lion. Battery-powered digital game calls include a wide selection of distress sounds as well as mountain lion vocalizations.

A good bet to hunt for cougars is to go where game is plentiful. Occasionally, a hunter may have an incidental sighting of a cougar that spurs a careful spot-and-stalk situation to avoid making the hunter the prey.

Some people question if lion meat is edible. The short answer is yes. Lion meat can be marinated then grilled, roasted, or even fried—all similar cooking methods of pork. But like boar and bear meat, lion meat can have trichinosis, so it must be cooked well. Treat all cooking methods like you would a prized cut of pork loin. Cougar meat can provide a "tasty and elegant meal." Like Ted Nugent says, "I enjoy eating cougar meat—now and then."

> **Note:** Mountain lion meat tastes similar to pork. However, the animal must be skinned as soon as possible and the meat well cared for. Old mountain men considered cougar meat a delicacy. Like bear and other predatory animals that hunt and eat other animals, make sure mountain lion meat is thoroughly cooked through to avoid contracting the trichinosis parasite.

MOUNTAIN LION STEAKS

SERVES 2

Soy-Sake Marinade

⅓ cup soy sauce

¼ cup sake

2 tablespoons water

2 tablespoons brown sugar

2 tablespoons mild chili sauce

2 cloves garlic, peeled and
    minced

1 teaspoon fresh ginger, minced

1 pinch salt

¼ teaspoon white pepper

Steaks

2 (8-ounce) mountain lion
    steaks

Flour, as needed

3 tablespoons of cooking oil

1 teaspoon bacon fat

In a bowl, combine the soy sauce, sake, water, brown sugar, chili sauce, garlic, ginger, salt, and pepper. Whisk until the brown sugar has dissolved.

Store the marinade in an airtight container in refrigerator until ready to use. The marinade will last for 5 to 7 days if stored properly.

Place the mountain lion steaks into a resealable plastic bag. Pour the Soy-Sake Marinade over the top, making sure all surfaces of meat are well coated. Seal bag and place into refrigerator for 2 or 3 hours.

Dry the steaks with flour by applying it to both the sides of the meat.

Pour the cooking oil in a large skillet over medium heat along with the bacon fat. Add the mountain lion steaks. Cook, turning occasionally, until the steaks are cooked through. (See note at the bottom of page 78 when cooking with mountain lion meat.)

Adapted from the recipe by Justin Ott, HuntingTipsandTricks.com.

WINE SUGGESTION:

Grgich Hills Estate Cabernet Sauvignon, Miljenko's Selection, Rutherford

The wine opens with concentrated aromas expressing characteristics of the famed Rutherford Dust. Flavors of red fruit along with blackberry, black currant, and elderberry play into the foreground, with dense tannins enveloping the palate. The mid-palate offers lingering undertones of dried herbs, graphite, and citrus that lead to a savory finish of bittersweet chocolate and tobacco.

WINE SUGGESTION:

Grgich Hills Estate Napa Valley Essence, Sauvignon Blanc

Using naturally occurring yeasts found on the grapes, Grgich Hills ferments the juice in 1,500-gallon French oak casks that are temperature-controlled for a cool fermentation to retain all the grape's delicate aromas. Then they select the best lots of the vintage and age the wine nine months in the same large oak casks. This wine displays aromas of lemon verbena, peach, and a hint of French vanilla on the nose. It is complex with great minerality and layered with balanced acidity. Pair it with pork loin, spicy foods, or these unique sausages.

MOUNTAIN LION FENNEL AND GARLIC SAUSAGE

MAKES ABOUT 5 POUNDS

4 pounds mountain lion loin, cold, cut into 1-inch chunks

1 pound pork shoulder, cold, cut into 1-inch chunks

1 pound pork fat, cold, cut into 1-inch chunks

2 tablespoons salt

1 tablespoon ground black pepper

2 tablespoons fennel seed

14 cloves garlic, peeled and finely chopped or pressed

½ cup apple cider vinegar

28–32mm hog casing (15–18 feet for a 5-pound batch)

In a bowl, add the mountain lion, pork shoulder, pork fat, salt, pepper, fennel, garlic, and vinegar. Mix well until completely blended and place in freezer for 30 minutes.

Immerse the hog casing in warm water.

Set up your meat grinder. Use a 3/16-inch grinder plate. Push the sausage mixture through the grinder, working quickly. If using the Kitchen Aid attachment, use it on level 4. Make sure the ground meat falls into a cold bowl. Next, slip a casing onto the stuffer tube, leaving a "tail" of at least 6 inches off the end. (Note: Run warm water through the sausage casings. This makes it easier to put the casings on the stuffer tube and lets you know if there are any holes in the casings). Add the meat to the stuffer and begin stuffing the mixture. Let the sausage come out in one long coil. When the sausage is all in the casings, tie off one end in a double knot, then pinch or twist the casing into 6-inch links, tying off the other end. Let the sausage links air-dry for 1 to 2 hours, then refrigerate until ready to cook. Note: This sausage mixture also makes excellent meatballs.

To Cook: These sausages are best when browned in a cast-iron skillet over medium heat; they take 10 to 12 minutes to cook completely. You can also place the sausages in a roasting pan and smother them with sauerkraut. Place the pan in a 400°F oven and bake, covered, for about 20 minutes. (See note at the bottom of page 78 when cooking with mountain lion meat.)

Adapted from the recipe by Field & Stream.

MOUNTAIN LION CHEESE-STUFFED MEATBALLS

MAKES ABOUT 20 (1½–2-INCH) MEATBALLS

1–1½ pounds finely ground
    mountain lion meat
2 eggs, beaten
1 cup fine breadcrumbs
2–3 tablespoons milk
1 teaspoon salt
½ teaspoon black pepper
Mozzarella cheese, as needed,
    cut into ¼-inch cubes
Vegetable oil, as needed, for
    frying

In a bowl, add the ground mountain lion meat, eggs, breadcrumbs, milk, salt, and pepper. Mix well by hand, but do not overmix. Roll into 1½- to 2-inch meatballs. While forming the meatballs, press one cube of cheese inside each ball. When all of the cheese-stuffed meatballs are formed, refrigerate for at least 1 hour before cooking.

Pour oil into a large skillet over medium heat. Allow the oil to heat for about 10 minutes. Then add the meatballs one-by-one, cooking in batches as to not overcrowd the pan. Fry the meatballs until brown and crisp on all sides, and the meat is thoroughly cooked through.

Adapted from the recipe by Justin Ott, HuntingTipsandTricks.com.

WINE SUGGESTION:

Grgich Hills Estate Chardonnay, Paris Tasting Commemorative

Initial citrus and flint stone notes on the nose open to peach and ripe mango, framed by subtle undertones of vanilla blossom. Fresh, yet fruit-forward and lush on the palate, well-integrated acidity carries secondary flavors of sweet stone fruit and melon. Oak nuances are beautifully integrated and give this wine unparalleled depth on the mid-palate followed by great minerality, salinity, and length.

PRONGHORN ANTELOPE

Antilocapra Americana

The pronghorn (a.k.a. American antelope) is also referred to as prongbuck and prairie antelope. Outfitters call pronghorns speed goats, goats, and prairie-racers. Whatever the term, the pronghorn, like mule deer, elk, bison, and mountain lion, are *icons* of the American west. Pronghorn antelope are not actually *antelope*. They were given the name because they looked like African antelope.

The pronghorn is indigenous to western North America. Its range extends from southwestern Canada, through the Great Plains, and into portions of Utah, Nevada, New Mexico, Montana, Wyoming, Colorado, Arizona, part of California, and northern Mexico.

The white fur on a pronghorn's throat, rump, side, and underside help easily identify it. An adult male is 4 to 5 feet long and about 3.5 feet high. Mature males can weigh from 90 to 145 pounds. Pronghorn, like bison, have horns—*not* antlers. Males, or bucks, have horns averaging 5 to 17 inches high. Females, or does, have horns that are rarely more than a few inches long.

What makes pronghorns unique, though, is their speed. They are the fastest land mammal in the Western hemisphere. Pronghorns have been clocked running between 35 to 55 mph. It is the second-fastest land animal to the African cheetah! Unlike cheetah, though, pronghorn evolved to *escape* predators, not *chase* prey.

Pronghorns prefer wide open, sprawling terrain but will inhabit areas with shrubs and trees, and, occasionally, can be found in mountain canyons, high extended mesas, and secluded benches in mountainous regions. Pronghorn eat a wide variety of plants. A favorite food group is forbs, which make up a majority of the pronghorn's diet. They also eat shrubs, grasses, and different types of cacti.

During the rut, adult males fiercely defend a particular area. They are territorial and mark their turf using scent and vocalizing. Females will mate with multiple males, often inciting fights between adult males.

Pronghorns are visible over long distances on open ground. Keep an eye out for tracks leading to and from water. Antelope rarely jump over fences, so look for tufts of hair caught in barbed wire under fences to help pinpoint well-used trails. The *primary* challenge of pronghorn hunting is to get close enough to these *very* wary and easily spooked animals to make an ethical long-distance kill shot—on a target that's only about 3½ feet high. Spot-and-stalk is a well-used tactic for hunting pronghorns. Hunters should use the landscape to hide their profile as they try to close the distance. Sneaking up on antelope often means having to crawl, which usually results in being stabbed with cactus thorns in the hands, elbows, stomach, and knees! If a hunter glasses an area for two days and fails to see any antelope, it would be best to move to another location.

One of the most exciting pronghorn hunting tactics is using decoys. Once a speed-goat is located, set up a decoy about 150 yards from it. By using an immature buck decoy, it will entice a mature buck in. The mature buck will come in thinking he can intimidate and run off the younger buck. Antelope decoying strategies can substantially kick up pronghorn hunting a few notches. A final, but important, key to successful pronghorn hunting boils down to using quality optics: a lightweight spotting scope, 10x40 binoculars, a rangefinder, and a 3-9x40mm rifle scope will help tremendously when trying to locate antelope across vast terrains.

Now comes the rub about antelope dinner-fare. First and foremost, the consensus by pronghorn hunters is *never* eat a rutting prongbuck. Like caribou, pronghorn meat can have a foul odor during cooking, which can affect the final flavor perception of a person's taste-buds. A buck not in rut, that was well cared for from field to table, will provide a fine wild game meal with an enjoyable flavor and tenderness unique to the animal.

ANTELOPE SUMMER SALAD
WITH LEMON VINAIGRETTE

SERVES 4–5

Lemon Vinaigrette

½ cup red wine vinegar

1 cup olive oil

3 tablespoons lemon juice

2 teaspoons honey

2 teaspoons salt

Freshly ground black pepper, to taste

Salad

1 pound boneless antelope loin or filets

Salt and cracked black pepper, to taste

1–2 heads romaine or green-leaf lettuce, cut into bite-sized pieces

2–3 cups arugula

1 red onion, peeled and sliced

1–2 cups cherry tomatoes, halved (or beefsteak, sliced and quartered)

Gorgonzola, Parmesan, or crumbled goat cheese, as needed

Toasted pecans or walnuts, as needed, optional

In a small bowl, whisk together the vinegar, oil, lemon juice, honey, salt, and pepper. Set aside this vinaigrette.

Preheat the oven to 425°F (or preheat an outdoor grill for direct, medium heat). Liberally season the antelope loin with salt and pepper. Roast or grill the loin to rare or medium-rare. For rare, remove the meat from the heat when the internal temperature from a meat thermometer reaches 115°F to 120°F. For medium-rare, remove when internal temperature reaches 120°F to 125°F. Remove from heat and let rest.

In a large bowl, add the lettuce, arugula, onion, tomatoes, cheese, and nuts. Drizzle with a little of the Lemon Vinaigrette over salad and toss.

To serve, arrange the salad among 4 or 5 serving plates. Thinly slice the loin across the grain and fan equal pieces on top of each salad.

Adapted from the recipe by Broken Arrow Ranch.

WINE SUGGESTION:

Grgich Hills Estate Chardonnay, Napa Valley

This Chardonnay opens to exuberant tropical aromatics of pineapple, green mango, and ripe peach, with underlying notes of dried herbs and Madagascar vanilla. While it is nimble on the attack, this wine quickly builds into a lush and fresh mid-palate, revisiting the tropical notes as well as adding citrus and lemon zest. A balanced acidity frames this impression perfectly and carries this wine into a long and complex finish that is both harmonious and vibrant.

CHICKEN FRIED ANTELOPE STEAK

SERVES 4

Vegetable oil or shortening, for
frying
2 cups flour
Salt and cracked black pepper,
as needed
2 pounds antelope or wild boar
cutlets (4–6 ounces each)
2 cups buttermilk

Cream Gravy
Pan drippings (from cooking
the cutlets above)
4 tablespoons flour
2 cups milk
Salt and cracked black pepper,
to taste

In a deep, heavy skillet add oil/shortening to a depth of about 2 inches. Heat the oil to 350°F. Lightly season the flour with salt and pepper. Dip the cutlets in the buttermilk and then dredge in the seasoned flour. Repeat this process again. Working in small batches, cook the cutlets in the oil, turning once, until brown, about 4 or 5 minutes total. Transfer to a baking sheet lined with paper towels to drain. The cooked steaks can be kept warm in a 200°F oven while the remaining steaks are cooked and the Cream Gravy is prepared.

Pour off all but 4 tablespoons of the drippings from the pan. Be sure to leave all the crunchy little particles in the pan. Add an equal amount of flour and stir while browning over medium-high heat. Continue cooking slowly and stirring while adding the milk. (Note: It's much easier to thin the gravy by adding more milk than it is to thicken the sauce by adding more flour, so add the milk slowly until the desired consistency is reached.) Season with salt and pepper, to taste.

Adapted from the recipe by Broken Arrow Ranch.

WINE SUGGESTION:

Grgich Hills Estate Cabernet Sauvignon, Napa Valley

Grgich's Napa Valley Cabernet entices the senses with layers of complex flavors that continue to evolve in the glass and on the palate. Aromas of black currants, violets, and plums dance in the glass, creating a new experience with every taste. The wine is artfully crafted, well-balanced, and lingers on the palate with a silky mouthfeel, leaving you craving for more. It pairs perfectly with barbecued ribs, a rack of lamb, or these antelope steaks.

HERB-CRUSTED ANTELOPE FILETS
WITH HORSERADISH SAUCE

SERVES 6–8

3–5 pounds boneless antelope
loin (or boneless leg filets)

2 tablespoons extra-virgin olive
oil

Kosher salt, to taste

4 tablespoons Dijon mustard,
divided

3 tablespoons cracked black
peppercorns

2 tablespoons finely chopped
fresh rosemary

2 tablespoons finely chopped
fresh thyme

Horseradish Sauce

¼ cup sour cream

¼ cup mayonnaise

¼ cup prepared horseradish

Rub the loin with olive oil then sprinkle a generous amount of salt over the loin. Next, rub the loin with 3 tablespoons of the mustard.

In a small bowl, combine the peppercorns, rosemary, and thyme. Mix well then season the loin with the herb mixture. Cover or wrap the loin with plastic and allow to sit at room temperature for 1 hour. Alternatively, the loin can also be seasoned in advance and placed in the refrigerator; remove the loin 1 hour before cooking.

Preheat the oven to 425°F (or preheat an outdoor grill for direct, medium heat).

Meanwhile, make the horseradish sauce by combining in a bowl the remaining 1 tablespoon mustard along with the sour cream, mayonnaise, and prepared horseradish. Mix well until smooth. Chill until ready to serve.

Roast or grill the loin to rare or medium-rare. For rare, remove the meat from the heat when the internal temperature from a meat thermometer reaches 115°F to 120°F, about 15 to 20 minutes total cooking time. For medium-rare, remove when internal temperature reaches 120°F to 125°F, about 20 to 25 minutes total cooking time. Remove from heat and let rest.

Slice the loin across the grain into ¼-inch medallions and serve with the horseradish sauce.

Adapted from the recipe by Broken Arrow Ranch.

WINE SUGGESTION:

Grgich Hills Estate Petit Verdot, Miljenko's Selection

Grgich maintains a cool fermentation temperature to preserve the rich fruit flavors and rely on open-top tanks to integrate oxygen with Petit Verdot's hardy tannins. Grgich aged this wine for almost two years in French oak barrels to allow the wood's harmonizing toast flavors to enhance the fruit. Its opulent aromas and flavors of luscious blackberries, soft leather, and hints of violets continue to become more complex in the glass. Match the wine's hearty flavors and sturdy tannins with grilled rib eye steak, wild game, or these antelope steaks.

WHITE-TAILED DEER

Odocoileus virginianus

Unquestionably, the white-tailed deer (a.k.a. Whitetail or Virginia Deer) is the most widely distributed and abundant big game animal in North America. According to the Wildlife Management Institute, the United States has between 12 to 14 million white-tailed deer. The whitetail's density levels vary from state-to-state. Lowest densities occur in arid states like Arizona, southern California, Nevada, New Mexico, and Utah.

Whitetails are the smallest deer within the North American family of deer. An adult buck is about 6.5 feet long and about 3.5 feet high at the shoulder. Depending on where it lives, and its diet, an adult whitetail buck can weigh between 90 to 300 pounds or more with most averaging 150 pounds (does weigh less, from 75 to 200 pounds).

Bucks have branching antlers with multiple tines (points). A buck grows a new set of antlers every year. Whitetails are most active at dusk and dawn but feed periodically during the day in undisturbed areas. A whitetail's home range encompasses about 640 square acres. During the rut, a buck's range can increase to three times that amount.

Whitetails are *the* most hunted big game animal in North America. Whitetails are so popular, it is the state animal of nine states. They are as flexible to what they eat as to where they live. As herbivores, they browse on over six hundred different plants. On occasion, they will graze on grasses. Some of their favorite foods include nuts, mushrooms, clovers, fruits, berries, twigs, buds, fungi, bark, grasses, leaves, and even poison ivy and sumac. Whitetails are fond of agricultural crops like alfalfa, soybeans, corn, grains, brassicas, and other legumes and almost anything else a farmer and/or a hunter plants in soil.

Whitetails are wary with excellent senses. Their sight is keen, particularly for detecting the slightest movement. Their eyes provide 310-degree vision—without the deer lifting its head. The whitetail's sense of smell and hearing are even keener survival tools. They can detect human odor and/or voices from hundreds of yards away. Whitetails make a variety of vocalizations including snorts, grunts, blats, bleats, and bawls to communicate with each other. They also use scent from more than a dozen glands to leave olfactory messages to other deer. When frightened, they can bound away at up to 30 miles per hour. Whitetails are also excellent swimmers and can swim up to 13 miles per hour.

To increase your hunting success, keep some basic points in mind. Always keep human scent to a bare minimum. When walking in the woods, avoid snapping branches, crunching dry leaves, and making heavy footfalls. Hunters can also use *pro-active* tactics like rattling, deer calling, decoying, making mock rubs, and scrapes and deer drives. Hunt in prime locations like thick stands of pines, swamps, marshes, river bottoms, ravines, and swales in fields. Savvy hunters know that when temperatures fall to single digits, whitetails will move throughout the day to various food sources. So, it's a good plan to take advantage of agricultural lands, planted food plots, and other current food sources.

Forget fast-food plant-based burgers; cook more venison burgers instead—they're healthier for you! The whitetail has filled countless hunters' freezers with untold pounds of high-quality venison. There is little doubt when it comes to eating big game meat that it's hard to beat the flavor, tenderness, and nutritional qualities of whitetail venison. It's a healthy red meat. In fact, a 3-ounce serving of roasted whitetail venison has about 135 calories, 130 grams of protein, fewer than 5 grams of fat, and only 3 to 5 grams of cholesterol.

Simply stated, a whitetail that has been properly field-dressed, butchered, and prepared will provide top-shelf table fare for family and friends and keep them coming back for more. Like all wild game, whitetail venison doesn't taste like beef and should *never* be compared to beef, pork, or the famed "chicken" remark. Deer venison, however, can be prepared like veal and/or lean beef. Like the most expensive steak, whitetail venison should be cooked rare to medium-rare to maximize its taste. Whitetail venison, Mother Nature's all-natural, antibiotic-free, grass-fed meat, will add an enjoyable dimension to your hunted meat table!

MULE DEER

Odocoileus hemionus

Mule deer and the American West go hand-in-hand. They are found in a wide variety of terrains throughout the western Great Plains and the Rocky Mountains. Mule deer can call almost any type of terrain home, including prairie lands, river bottoms, mature aspen forests, grasslands, farmlands, and alpine ridgetops above the timber line. They also inhabit large expanses of arid southwest, cactus-strewn deserts, deep canyonlands, and gorges. Essentially, mule deer are found in almost any environment from the Alaskan coastal islands, down to southern Baja Mexico.

Mule deer got their name because their ears resemble the ears of a mule or donkey. Therein lies the stigma attached to them; they are often referred to as "dumb" game. They may be slightly less hypersensitive than white-tailed deer, but by no means should they be considered easy to hunt. Experienced hunters say a mature mule buck is as wary and difficult to hunt as any savvy whitetail buck.

Mule deer are the second most hunted deer species and *among* the top five most hunted big game animals in North America. A mature buck can easily weigh 300 pounds, have a set of heavy forking (bifurcated) antlers that can be 30 inches wide, and have 10 or more long points!

Most hunting for mule deer takes place throughout the Rocky Mountain states (Idaho, Nevada, New Mexico, Montana, Wyoming, Colorado, Utah, and Arizona). There's an old adage about hunting mule deer: If at day's end, a hunter's eyes don't ache from using binoculars to locate mule deer, they didn't glass long enough! Glassing is a prime tactic, particularly from high vantage points overlooking vast open expanses. Careful glassing can reveal bedded bucks. Be sure to cover each piece of habitat carefully to increase the number of bucks seen. Soon after sunrise, begin to vigilantly glass shaded areas. Adult bucks bed down quickly after sunup under pines and brush. Pay equal attention to any ledge outcroppings that offer seclusion and shade.

After spending a few hours in the morning glassing likely terrain, one can start stalk hunting. Stalking mule deer is often an overlooked but prime mule deer tactic that can yield excellent opportunities to kill a trophy. Experienced bucks also bed down in deep, narrow, twisting gullies, steep canyon hillsides, brushy draws, deep swales, and other similar terrain. A hunter could get a chance at kicking up a good buck from its midday bed in such areas. The key is to proceed slowly and carefully and *always* be at the ready to shoot. Additionally, don't overlook hunting the flat plains, especially after the season progresses. Many a dandy mule buck are taken in flat lower grounds far from mountainous areas.

When it comes to eating mule deer venison, it can be as fine tasting as any whitetail. This is especially true for mule deer living in agricultural lands, high country areas, and river bottoms. Deer living in scrub oaks, deserts, sage brush, and similar terrains, however, can have meat that is flavored like the foods they eat. That's categorically true when their diet is *primarily* sage brush, making the meat taste exceptionally strong.

During the peak of the rut, a mule deer buck's meat can certainly have a stronger gamey taste than whitetail venison. In general, though, mule deer venison can be excellent table fare albeit it does have a more pronounced wild game flavor. The key to ensure good tasting mule deer meat is to field dress it quickly and properly. Like any wild game meat, it doesn't taste like beef, so good field care, proper butchering, and preparing mule deer venison is *the* key to a flavorful meat experience.

>>>

WINE SUGGESTION:

2018 DeLille Cellars Roussanne

Light honey colored in appearance, 2018 Roussanne shows aromas of cantaloupe, peach, and nectarine, tempered by appealing savory notes of salinity and cucumber skin. Lively and bright on the palate, fruit flavors are dominated by pear and green apple, with key lime to add interest. Some extended lees contact contributes a hint of creamy brioche character, adding body and sweetness to the finish, all wrapped in firm tannin.

VENISON STIR-FRY

SERVES 4

¼ cup dry sherry

1½ tablespoons finely chopped fresh peeled ginger

2 cloves garlic, peeled and finely chopped

1 tablespoon sesame oil

¼ cup soy sauce

1 orange, zested

12 ounces venison, cut into stir-fry strips

1 teaspoon cornstarch

1 tablespoon peanut oil

1 cup broccoli, cut into bite-sized pieces

1 medium carrot, peeled and sliced on the bias

1 medium onion, peeled and cut into 8 wedges

½ medium red bell pepper, seeded and cut into pieces

½ medium yellow bell pepper, seeded and cut into pieces

10 mushroom caps, halved

1 cup snow peas, ends trimmed

4 cups cooked rice

¼ cup thinly sliced scallions, for garnish

1 teaspoon toasted sesame seeds, for garnish

Prepare the marinade by combining, in a large bowl or gallon-sized sealable plastic bag, the sherry, ginger, garlic, sesame oil, soy sauce, and orange zest. Stir to blend and add the venison. Squeeze out the air and seal the bag. Marinate the venison for up to 2 hours at room temperature or longer in the refrigerator, turning the bag occasionally. Allow the meat to remain at room temperature 30 minutes before cooking.

Strain the marinade into a measuring cup and add enough water to make ⅓ cup liquid. Add the cornstarch and stir to dissolve.

Heat a nonstick wok or large nonstick skillet over high heat. Add the peanut oil and venison. Stir-fry until the venison loses its red color, about 1 to 2 minutes. Remove the venison with a slotted spoon. Reserve and keep warm.

Stir in the broccoli and carrots. Cover and steam for 1 minute. Uncover and stir in the onion, peppers, and mushrooms. Stir-fry another 3 minutes. Add the snow peas, browned venison, and the reserved marinade/water mixed with cornstarch. Stir continuously until the sauce begins to thicken, about 2 minutes.

To serve, spoon the venison and vegetables over cooked rice. Garnish with a sprinkle of scallions and toasted sesame seeds.

Adapted from the recipe by Broken Arrow Ranch.

VENISON BOLOGNESE WITH FETTUCINE

SERVES 4

1 pound ground venison

1 clove garlic, peeled and minced

½ teaspoon vegetable-flavored bouillon powder

1½ cups peeled and chopped onion

1 teaspoon salt

1 (8-ounce) can tomato paste

2 teaspoons Worcestershire sauce

2 teaspoons red wine vinegar

½ teaspoon **each** Tabasco, basil, rosemary, marjoram, fresh ground black pepper

1½ teaspoons **each** oregano, chili powder, paprika, sugar

1 bay leaf

1½ cups chopped green pepper

4 ounces fresh mushrooms, sliced ¼-inch thick

½ cup fresh Italian flat-leaf parsley, minced

Fettucine, cooked to package instructions

Spray a large pan with nonstick spray and brown the venison and garlic over medium heat. Set aside. Mix the bouillon powder with ¾ cup water and add the onion. Heat in a microwave or on the stove until the onion is soft.

In large, heavy pot, add the salt, tomato paste, Worcestershire, vinegar, Tabasco, basil, rosemary, marjoram, black pepper, oregano, chili powder, paprika, sugar, bay leaf, green pepper, mushrooms, and parsley. Mix well, then add the venison, onion, garlic, and bouillon. Simmer slowly over low heat for 1½ to 2 hours.

Remove bay leaf. Serve over fettucine.

Adapted from the recipe by Broken Arrow Ranch.

WINE SUGGESTION:

2017 DeLille Cellars D2

The D2 offers abundant dried cranberry and raspberry aromas surging from the glass, with intertwined darker fruit notes of cassis, blueberry, and blackberry. Delicately balanced oak influence contributes cocoa and coffee bean notes while remaining completely respectful of the fruit. This appealing wine is vibrant and extraordinarily fresh on the palate, with persistent fruit flavors of pomegranate and blueberry. Understated and subtle tannin provides welcome structure, while excellent early integration offers accessibility, generosity, and abundant pleasure despite the wine's youth.

VENISON CURRY

SERVES 6

3 tablespoons vegetable oil

1 cup chopped onion

2 tablespoons ground coriander

1½ teaspoons ground cumin

1 teaspoon ground cardamom

1 teaspoon ground ginger

1 teaspoon ground turmeric

¼ teaspoon cracked black pepper

⅛ teaspoon ground red pepper

2 cloves garlic, peeled and minced

2 pounds venison, cleaned, trimmed, and cut into bite-size pieces

1 (14-ounce) can beef broth

1 cup water

1 teaspoon salt

¼ cup plain yogurt

1 teaspoon fresh lemon juice

6 cups cooked rice

In a large sauté pan, heat the oil over medium-high heat until hot. Add the onion and sauté until soft and golden. Reduce the heat to low, and add the coriander, cumin, cardamom, ginger, turmeric, black pepper, red pepper, and garlic. Stir for 1 minute. Increase the heat to medium and add the venison. Stir frequently until meat is browned. Add the broth, water, and salt. Cover and simmer until the meat is tender, about 2 hours. Uncover and let the sauce thicken, about 20 minutes. Reduce the heat to stop the boiling action and add the yogurt and lemon juice. Stir until well incorporated. Remove from heat.

To serve, place 1 cup of cooked rice on each serving dish. Divide the Venison Curry and spoon over the rice. Arrange the garnishes around the table so each person can add the garnish(es) of their choice.

Garnishes: chutney, chopped scallions, grated hard-boiled eggs, sliced almonds, chopped cucumbers, chopped bananas, coconut, raisins, fresh cilantro, and crumbled bacon pieces.

Adapted from the recipe by Broken Arrow Ranch.

WINE SUGGESTION:

2018 DeLille Cellars Rosé

Presenting a beautiful pink coral color, the Grenache-dominated 2018 Rosé showcases a nose of kiwi, melon, and light red raspberry. Bright citrus flavors join dried strawberry, peach, and hints of dried tarragon and dill in the mouth. Perfectly dry and brilliantly crisp, this wine has a substantial finish capped by a generous tropical guava flavor.

WILD BOAR

Sus scrofa

Wild pig first appeared in the United States as a result of domestic swine escaping from early European explorers. In the early 1900s, Eurasian Russian wild boars were released into hunting preserves and, where both boars coexisted, the two species interbred. Today, many hybrid populations exist throughout the country. Hunting wild boar is a popular game sport and accounts for the expansion of its range throughout the United States and Puerto Rico. Recently, wild pigs have begun to populate throughout the Northeast. According to the latest census, there are about seven million wild boars inhabiting forty-five states.

Wild boars (a.k.a. feral swine, hogs, razorbacks, or porkers) adapt quickly to a wide array of climates, terrains, vegetation, and other conditions, allowing for greater range expansion and population increases. Wild hogs have no natural predators (other than humans) to keep their numbers in balance. They flourish in almost *any* habitat other than true arid deserts. As opportunistic feeders, boars forage on almost anything. Some preferred foods include acorns, forbs, tubers, browse, fruits, and bulbs with their *favorite* foods being wild mushrooms and agricultural crops. Wild pigs are voracious feeders and will eat a food source until they have totally exhausted it.

A typical boar can measure 5 to 6 feet from nose to tail and is about 2½ feet tall at the shoulder. Females are smaller and generally weigh about 150 to 170 pounds. Males usually weigh about 200 to 225 pounds but can weigh as much as 400 pounds or more. Wild boars are active throughout the day and night and have an inherent instinct for routine behaviors, utilizing the same trails to and from food sources and bedding places.

When hunting wild boar, caution is definitely recommended. These feral animals are very unpredictable and have extremely short fuses. Hunting feral hogs can be more hazardous than pursuing grizzly bears. Male boars won't hesitate to charge (attack) anything perceived as a threat. Females do the same, but mostly to protect their piglets. Boars use their razor-sharp tusks as aptly and lethally as the Three Musketeers used their swords to disembowel an opponent.

Wild boars are hunted for sport and their tasty meat. Without question, Texas is the top choice to harvest *free-ranging* wild pigs. Other states include California, Hawaii, South Carolina, Oklahoma, Alabama, Arkansas, Louisiana, Georgia, and Florida. Many private hunting preserves throughout the country offer boar hunting, too.

Successful boar hunts start with knowing their habits and behaviors. They are very intelligent land animals, so using strategic tactics is a key element to success. It is important to learn how to decipher boar tracks to locate a sounder (a group of wild hogs). Once found, applying stealth to get close to a sounder is crucial. As wild pigs have thick hides, it is imperative to use a loadout capable of effective penetration.

The best times to hunt wild boar is generally at dusk and dawn. During the winter, hogs may feed in open areas all day. Hogs are vulnerable when they are feeding. To locate wild pigs, know what current food sources they are feeding on and where their bedding areas are located. Wild hogs also respond very well to predator calls. Hunters should learn how to mimic a wounded rabbit or other wounded small-game animal. Hogs will even respond well to the sounds of a fawn deer in distress.

As anyone who has eaten wild boar will testify, it doesn't taste like domestic pork or "chicken." Wild boar meat has a concentrated pork flavor that's sweet and nutty and has also been likened to a combination of beef and domestic pork. It is slightly darker, leaner, higher in protein, and has less cholesterol than domestic pork, making it a healthier meat. Generally, about half the live weight will end up being boneless meat, which can be as succulent as any quality cut of domestic pork. It is advised by the CDC to cook wild pork "thoroughly." By cooking this lean meat to 165 degrees, it will kill potential harmful bacteria and/or trichinosis.

WILD BOAR PORCHETTA

SERVES 6–8

4 tablespoons olive oil

1 onion, peeled and thinly sliced

1 fennel bulb, thinly sliced

¾ pound Italian sausage (or wild boar Italian sausage)

2 tablespoons fennel seeds

2 tablespoons cracked black pepper

2 tablespoons fresh rosemary, chopped (or ½ tablespoon dried)

6 cloves garlic, peeled and chopped

Fennel leaves, chopped

2 eggs, beaten

4 pounds wild boar shoulder roast (or a rolled and tied wild boar leg)

Salt and pepper, to taste

4 cups vegetable mix, coarsely chopped (onion, celery, carrots, parsnips, etc.)

4 tablespoons butter, melted

4 tablespoons olive oil

In a large sauté pan over medium-high heat, add the olive oil. When hot, add the onion and fennel (bulb only). Cook until the onion is soft and translucent. Add the sausage, fennel seeds, pepper, rosemary, and garlic. Cook about 10 minutes, stirring frequently so the garlic does not burn. Allow the mixture to cool, then mix in the chopped fennel leaves and eggs.

Preheat the oven to 350°F.

Spread the mixture over one side of the wild boar then roll it up with a truss of kitchen twine. Spread the vegetable mixture on the bottom of a large roasting pan. Note: Use a mix of sturdy, savory vegetables to keep the wild boar off the bottom of the pan. Set the boar on top of the vegetable mix. Combine the 4 tablespoons melted butter with the olive oil. Roast in the oven until the internal temperature reaches 150°F, about 2 to 2½ hours, basting every 20 to 30 minutes with melted butter and olive oil mixture. When done, remove from the oven and let rest for 15 to 20 minutes. Then slice thickly and serve.

Adapted from the recipe by Broken Arrow Ranch.

WINE SUGGESTION:

2017 DeLille Cellars D2

The D2 offers abundant dried cranberry and raspberry aromas surging from the glass, with intertwined darker fruits notes of cassis, blueberry, and blackberry. Delicately balanced oak influence contributes cocoa and coffee bean notes while remaining completely respectful of the fruit. This appealing wine is vibrant and extraordinarily fresh on the palate, with persistent fruit flavors of pomegranate and blueberry. Understated and subtle tannin provides welcome structure, while excellent early integration offers accessibility, generosity, and abundant pleasure despite the wine's youth.

ROASTED WILD BOAR LEG
WITH MUSTARD CAPER SAUCE

SERVES 8–10

1 (5- to 6-pound) bone-in boar
    leg
2 tablespoons olive oil
⅓ cup Dijon mustard

Mustard Caper Sauce
6 tablespoons butter
½ cup dry white wine
2 tablespoons Dijon mustard
½ teaspoon Worcestershire
    sauce
3 tablespoons capers, well
    drained

Remove the boar leg from the refrigerator and bring to room temperature (about 1 hour before cooking). Transfer the leg to a rack set in a large roasting pan.

Preheat the oven to 450°F.

In a small bowl, combine the olive oil and mustard, and spread liberally all over the boar leg. Add a little water in the roasting pan and place in the oven. Roast for 20 minutes. Reduce the oven temperature to 275°F and continue cooking the leg until a meat thermometer inserted into the thickest part of the leg reads 150°F, about 4 to 5 hours.

Transfer the leg to a cutting board. Tent with foil and let rest for about 30 minutes before carving.

To make the Mustard Caper Sauce, in a saucepan or pot, melt the butter over low heat. Mix in the wine, mustard, Worcestershire sauce, and capers. Stir to blend.

To serve, spoon the sauce over the sliced boar meat.

Adapted from the recipe by Broken Arrow Ranch.

WINE SUGGESTION:

2017 DeLille Cellars Four Flags

The 2017 Four Flags shows elegance and restraint on the nose. Initially tightly wound and impenetrable, fruit begins to emerge—blue and red aromas of cranberry, blueberries, and anise, with alluring black tea, gravel, and cedar adding refinement. Absolutely enclosed by generous oak, ample fruit seeps through, delivering the savory balance Red Mountain typifies. A long finish carried by persistent and building tannin offers great promise for the future.

WILD BOAR POZOLE

SERVES 6–8

3 pounds wild boar, cleaned, trimmed, and cubed

Flour, as needed

Olive oil, as needed

3 quarts chicken or pork broth, divided

2 poblano chilis, or 1 (7-ounce) can diced green chilis

3 (13-ounce) cans hominy, drained (white, yellow, or mixed)

1 medium onion, peeled and chopped

8 cloves garlic, peeled and minced

3 dried New Mexico (Anaheim) chilis, ground (or 2 tablespoons chili powder)

½ teaspoon dried oregano

½ teaspoon cracked black pepper

Salt, as needed

Sour cream, optional

Scallions, chopped, optional

Lightly coat the wild boar cubes with flour. Knock off any excess flour. In a large sauté pan or pot, heat some olive oil over medium-high heat. When hot, add the boar cubes in small batches, and brown on all sides. Once all the cubes are browned, deglaze the pan/pot with a small amount of broth, scraping up all the bits, and add this mixture to your cooking vessel.

Meanwhile, roast the poblano chilis: Broil the chilis 2 or 3 inches below the coils in a rimmed baking pan or roasting pan until the skins are nicely charred, about 7 minutes. Flip the chilis over and broil about 5 minutes longer until the other side is also charred. Remove from the oven and drape some foil over the chilis for about 10 minutes. This will make skinning the chilis much easier. Remove the skin, stems, and seeds, and discard. Rinse the chilis and then chop.

In a large pot or Dutch oven, add the wild boar cubes along with the hominy, onion, garlic, dried ground chilis, the roasted poblano chilis, oregano, pepper, and the remaining broth. Bring the mixture to a boil then cover and gently simmer until the wild boar is fork-tender, about 2 hours. Add salt to taste.

Serve in bowls garnished with sour cream and chopped scallions, if desired.

Adapted from the recipe by Broken Arrow Ranch.

WINE SUGGESTION:

2018 DeLille Cellars Roussanne

Light honey colored in appearance, 2018 Roussanne shows aromas of cantaloupe, peach, and nectarine, tempered by appealing savory notes of salinity and cucumber skin. Lively and bright on the palate, fruit flavors are dominated by pear and green apple, with key lime to add interest. Some extended lees contact contributes a hint of creamy brioche character, adding body and sweetness to the finish, all wrapped in firm tannin.

UPLAND BIRDS & WATERFOWL

MOURNING DOVE

Zenaida macroura

Mourning Dove (a.k.a. American Mourning Dove, rain dove) is a member of the family *Columbidae*. It is the most popular upland gamebird in the United States. Doves are protected under the Migratory Bird Treaty Act. Over the past few years, according to the US Fish and Wildlife Service, hunters shot more than 10 million doves per year. Doves are legal game in almost all states, other than a few that protect doves as listed "songbirds." For the sake of brevity, although there are other subspecies of doves, they're not the focus here.

The mourning dove's range is extensive, covering nearly 4,200,000 square miles! In North America, doves are found in all of the continental United States, most of Mexico, and most of southern Canada. Doves are found in open and semi-open environments, farms, grasslands, prairielands and second growth woods.

Mourning doves, males and females, look very similar. They make several different types of vocalizations, including a raspy or rattling sound made prior to cooing, nesting, greeting, and alarm calls. Mourning doves are medium-sized birds about 11 to 13 inches long and weigh between 4 and 6 ounces. They are very strong fliers and can reach speeds of 50 miles per hour or more. A mourning dove's ability to make instant and amazing aerodynamic maneuvers is generally uncontested. Their speed, shape, nimbleness, and dazzling flying capabilities all add to their mystique of being tough targets for gunners.

Mourning doves' favorite "eats" include all types of weed seeds. Numerous concentrations of doves are always found near harvested grain fields. Doves must have water daily. Watering sites are as attractive to doves as nectar is to bees. Hunters that locate fresh-standing watering sites will be paid handsomely with large concentrations of doves flying in and out to drink.

Dove hunters must keep a close eye on the weather, which is a primary concern for dove movement. Rain and strong winds significantly reduce movement. Well-concealed hunting blinds are an absolute necessity. A blind that is not well-camouflaged will wise up doves to the hunt lickety-split. The savvy dove hunter has a stash of dove decoys. Place them in plain view and the decoys will draw in birds like a fox to a hen house. Another tactic is to use dove calls. Both decoys and calls add an element of realism doves find hard to ignore. Knowing where doves can drink will provide peak action at dawn and dusk.

Dove hunters often choose a gun with more firepower than is needed. Instead of using a heavy, long-barreled 12-gauge that is cumbersome, a better choice would be a lightweight 16-, 20-, or even a 28-gauge shotgun with a 26-inch barrel and #7½ or #8 shot shells.

The wise dove hunter practices good field care. Pluck the birds as soon as possible. Dove feathers come off easily. Remove the entrails and blood from the chest cavity and then put the dressed doves whole on ice in a portable cooler. Alternatively, you can breast them out by separating the breast from the back, wings, and feet and then ice them in the cooler. Either way is going to assure a better-tasting bird.

From field to plate, doves make good-eating table fare, but that's only if they are prepared correctly. Doves can be oven-baked, seared over a charcoal grill, pan-fried, or roasted whole. As with all game birds, if the skin is left on, it will help to retain the natural juices. Doves dislike being overcooked; it dries out the meat. Most hunters take the breasts off, wrap them in bacon with a jalapeño, and grill them—but, by far, that isn't the only way to prepare doves. One dove is a good portion for an appetizer, and three to four are required for a main course.

As a side note, some folks refer to dove as squab. Squab is a small, subtle bird that is considered quite coveted, sophisticated, and distinctive in most western cuisines. Called "the bird of royalty," squab has been popular among members of the French nobility as far back as the Middle Ages and enjoyed in cuisines as far back as ancient Egypt.

In culinary terminology, however, squab is a young domestic pigeon, typically under four weeks old. The meat is widely described as tasting like dark (yup, you guessed it again) chicken. Prior to the current practice of raising one type of pigeon specifically for meat consumption, mourning doves had also been included as squab.

BACON-WRAPPED JALAPEÑO DOVE POPPERS

SERVES 2–4 AS A MAIN COURSE, 8–10 AS AN APPETIZER

15 whole dove breasts (or 30 single breasts), cleaned

Garlic salt, as needed

Freshly cracked black pepper, as needed

1 package (8 ounces) softened cream cheese

15 jalapeño slices (fresh or canned)

2 (16-ounce) packages sliced bacon, cut in half

Preheat an outdoor barbecue, using either mesquite wood, oak, or charcoal.

Begin by prepping the dove breasts. If they are still on the bone, use a sharp paring knife to separate the breasts from the breastbones to make 30 lobes. Next, lightly season with the garlic salt and pepper. Spread some cream cheese on each breast, followed by one jalapeño slice, and wrap in bacon. Secure the bacon with a toothpick.

Arrange the wrapped dove breasts on the barbecue. Grill for 3 to 5 minutes, then turn over and continue grilling until the bacon is crisp and the dove is cooked through. Remove from grill and serve warm.

Adapted from the recipe by Patricia Sharpe and Texas Monthly.

WINE SUGGESTION:

Duckhorn Vineyards Napa Valley Chardonnay

The recent growing seasons, particularly 2017, yielded an intense and complex expression of Napa Valley Chardonnay, with alluring aromas of nectarine, yellow plum, pineapple upside-down cake, and sweet spices. On the palate, zesty acidity and an underlying silkiness add depth and nuance, with French oak–inspired hints of vanilla, sweet dough, and clove framing the generous fruit.

CHARLIE'S WILD DOVE

SERVES 4

4 thick strips smoked bacon, chopped

1 small white onion, peeled and chopped (about 1 cup)

1 small carrot, peeled and chopped (about 1 cup)

½ large celery stalk, chopped (about 1 cup)

Salt and black pepper, to taste

2 cups white wine

1½ cups chicken stock

2 tablespoons chopped fresh sage

2 tablespoons chopped fresh rosemary

4 doves

4 thick slices sourdough bread

Heat a Dutch oven and add the bacon. Cook until the bacon is crisp, about 8 minutes. Remove the bacon and set aside. Add the onion, carrot, celery, salt, and pepper to the pot. Season and sauté in the bacon fat until they start to caramelize, about 6 minutes. Add the wine and chicken stock and deglaze the pot. Add the sage and rosemary. Bring to a simmer and add the dove breasts. Cover and poach about 10 minutes if using the breasts or 14 minutes if using the whole bird. Remove the doves, strain the chicken stock, and season to taste. Place a thick slice of sourdough bread in each bowl, place the doves on top, ladle the poaching liquid over, and sprinkle with bacon.

Adapted from the recipe by Chef John Ash and James O. Fraioli from the cookbook Culinary Birds.

WINE SUGGESTION:

Duckhorn Vineyards Napa Valley Merlot

A classic expression of Napa Valley Merlot, this wine offers alluring aromas of lush cherry, raspberry, cocoa, and freshly baked pie crust. The cherry and raspberry notes are echoed on the silky palate, where fine-grained tannins and flavors of ripe plum, blueberry, licorice, and subtle baking spice draw the wine to a long, elegant finish.

DOVE SARDINIAN STYLE

SERVES 6

3 large doves
1 small onion, sliced
2 medium carrots, chopped
1 large stalk celery, sliced
6 anchovy fillets
2 large bay leaves
2 cups dry white wine
Chicken stock
1 cup extra virgin olive oil
¼ cup white wine vinegar
3 tablespoons finely chopped
   parsley
2 tablespoons chopped drained
   capers
Salt and freshly ground black
   pepper

Rinse the birds, and place in a pan just large enough to hold them in a single layer. Strew the onions, carrots, celery, anchovies, and bay leaves in the bottom of a saucepan just large enough to hold the birds in a single layer, then add the wine and enough stock to cover. Bring to a simmer and then cover the pan and cook gently for 45 minutes, or until birds are very tender.

Make the sauce by whisking the olive oil, vinegar, parsley and capers together and seasoning to your taste with salt and pepper. Remove the birds from the pan, cut them in half lengthwise, and arrange them on a serving dish. Remove the bay leaves and pour the sauce over and allow to cool before serving.

Note: Strain and save the stewing liquid for other uses.

Adapted from the recipe by Chef John Ash and James O. Fraioli from the cookbook Wild.

WINE SUGGESTION:

Duckhorn Vineyards Napa Valley Sauvignon Blanc

This vibrant Sauvignon Blanc begins with enticing aromas of lemongrass, lychee, passionfruit, melon, and pineapple, followed by hints of white nectarine and lime. On the juicy palate, a subtle viscosity is perfectly balanced by refreshing acidity that adds precision to the citrus and tropical fruit flavors, while driving the wine to a bright, zesty finish.

RUFFED GROUSE

Bonasa umbellus

Of the fourteen subspecies of grouse, the Ruffed Grouse is the *primary* species that is best known, widely distributed, most hunted, and the best table fare of all grouse. Following the Ruffed Grouse in the order of hunting popularity and table fare is the Ptarmigan, Sharp-tailed, Dusky, Sooty, Spruce, and Sage, and the lesser and greater Prairie Chicken subspecies of grouse. The differences between them are negligible and have more to do with where they live and their weight.

The Ruffed Grouse (a.k.a. drummer or thunder-chicken) is often incorrectly called a partridge, prairie chicken, or even a pheasant—all of which are names appropriately belonging to other upland birds. Ruffed Grouse are found across the northern part of the United States, parts of the Rocky Mountains, Pacific Northwest, and into Alaska, but are much more widespread in the Northeast, New England, and the upper Midwest.

Ruffed Grouse measure about 15 to 20 inches from tail to beak and weigh about 1½ pounds. They are covered with a mixture of feathers effectively colored to camouflage the bird from predators. Ruffed Grouse prefer mixed woodlands, shrubs, farmlands, brambles, and herbaceous vegetation, where they forage for acorns, seeds, buds, leaves, fruits, catkins, some ferns, twigs, clover, strawberries, waste grain, and insects.

Ruffed Grouse utilize even the slightest cover to the maximum. They have an instinct to position themselves, so an obstruction separates them from predators, particularly from hunters. If that isn't frustrating enough, they will almost always flush out of the other side of whatever cover is safeguarding them from danger. The consistently successful ruffed grouse hunter is able to define would-be escape routes before the ruffed grouse flushes.

Experienced Ruffed Grouse hunters locate signs to find birds. Like deer, they use trails through the underbrush where they drop feathers along the edges. Locate areas where there is gravel and green clover. Grouse frequently seek both along farm roads and dirt roads in the early morning and late afternoon. Still-hunt these areas to flush birds. Like wild turkey, grouse also use sandy areas to dust their feathers. Birds will return to these spots during the late afternoon to dust and to socialize.

While Ruffed Grouse look big, they are fairly easy birds to bring down. Small shot, size 7½ or 8 is usually all that is needed for Ruffed Grouse. A 16- or 20-gauge pump with a 26- or 28-inch barrel is an ideal grouse gun. All the typical barrel configuration choices (autoloaders, side-by-sides, pumps, and over/unders) are best left up to the hunter.

Ruffed Grouse rates high among the top tier of fine-tasting wild fowl. Among upland game hunters, Ruffed Grouse is acclaimed to be the best tasting of all the grouse species. Its meat is definitely whiter, and it has a more delicate, milder flavor than most upland gamebirds. Ruffed Grouse could easily replace just about any chicken dish that highlights preparing chicken breasts. In fact, Ruffed Grouse has the same proportion of dark and white meat as chicken. The meat tends to lean toward being sweet-tasting and tender. Many hunters claim grouse meat is as good as any game bird gets. While some ol' timers still like to hang their game birds (and deer) out to "age" for several weeks, this process of aging only decays the meat, particularly on small game birds, ruining their inherent flavor and tenderness. Ruffed Grouse is said by many to be a pleasant, full-flavored wild game. It requires a much shorter cooking time than other fowl, including domestic chicken. Many experienced hunters of all types of fowl claim Ruffed Grouse even surpasses the flavor and tenderness of pheasant.

SHARP-TAILED GROUSE
Tympanuchus phasianellus
The Sharp-tailed Grouse (a.k.a. sharp-tail or fire grouse) is about 18 inches long and typically weighs about 2 pounds. They are mostly vegetarians but do eat insects. Sharp-tails are found in the Rocky Mountains, Great Plains, and the Midwest. Hunters need only to station themselves along known sharp-tailed flight paths and wait for incoming birds. The meat is very dark and red. Cooked on the rare side, Sharp-tailed Grouse rates a close second to Ruffed Grouse.

SPRUCE GROUSE
Falcipennis canadensis
Spruce Grouse (a.k.a. Canada grouse) is a medium-sized grouse about 16 inches long and weighs in at less than 2 pounds. It is found from Alaska to the Pacific Northwest and across the northern states from Idaho to Maine. This species prefers to walk on the ground or along tree limbs rather than fly. When it flies, it only covers short distances, mostly from the ground to a nearby tree branch. It is said Canada grouse makes excellent table fare because it mainly eats insects, herbs, and berries—not pine needles or sagebrush.

DUSKY GROUSE
Dendragapus obscurus
Dusky Grouse are found throughout the Rocky Mountains, parts of California's Sierra Mountains, and even in Eastern Alaska. Dusky Grouse are about 20 inches long and weigh about 4 pounds. It is a close relative of the sooty grouse. Both were previously considered a single species, the blue grouse. The breast of a Dusky Grouse can be tender and flavorful. The legs and the rest of the bird have a more pronounced gamey taste.

SOOTY GROUSE

Dendragapus fuliginosus

The Sooty Grouse is a forest-dweller native to North America's Pacific Coast. It measures between 15 and 20 inches and weighs about 2½ pounds. It is a close relative of the Dusky Grouse. The two were previously considered a single species. The male has black feathers. It forages on beetles, grasshoppers, ants, pine needles, and other green plants. Sooty doesn't taste like Ruffed Grouse; yet, it isn't as gamey as some hunters claim it is.

THE GREATER SAGE GROUSE

Centrocercus urophasianus

Sage Grouse (a.k.a. sage hen) are the largest grouse species. They live in all sagebrush or juniper environments in Wyoming, California, Oregon, Idaho, Nevada, Utah, Montana, Colorado, and the western Dakotas. Adult males are 26 to 30 inches long and weigh 4 to 7 pounds. I mentioned earlier that nearly all hunted game tastes like what it eats. This generally applies to what most hunters say, that Sage Grouse tastes like and has an aroma of sagebrush. I have never eaten sagebrush so I can't make any comparisons.

PAN-SEARED GROUSE WITH SMOKED BARLEY RISOTTO AND CRANBERRY GASTRIQUE

SERVES 4

2 cups all-purpose brine (¼ cup kosher salt, ¼ cup sugar, 2 cups water)

4 grouse breasts, cleaned with skin on

2 tablespoons brown sugar

2 tablespoons pomegranate juice

Canola oil, as needed

½ cup barley

4½ cups chicken stock

2 teaspoons kosher salt

1 teaspoon freshly cracked black pepper

1 teaspoon liquid smoke (only use if you do not have a smoker available)

¾ cup shaved Parmesan cheese

Minced chives, for garnish, if desired

Begin by making the brine. In a saucepot over high heat, add the salt, sugar, and water. Bring to a boil, then boil for 5 minutes. Remove from heat and chill in the refrigerator. Once the brine is completely cool, arrange the grouse breasts in a baking dish and pour the brine over the top of the breasts. Let marinate in the refrigerator for at least 4 hours, but no more than 8 hours or the grouse will be too salty.

Next, create the Cranberry Gastrique by placing the brown sugar in a small saucepan along with just enough water to hydrate. (Note: If you add too much water, don't worry. All the water will dissipate.) Caramelize the sugar over low heat just until the sugar begins to bubble, then add the pomegranate juice. Return to a simmer for 5 minutes, then remove from the heat and allow to cool completely.

If using an outdoor smoker, at this point set your smoker to 200°F. Place the barley flat on a smoking tray, and smoke for 20 minutes. If you do not have a smoker, don't worry, you can substitute later with liquid smoke.

To make the Smoked Barley Risotto, place a medium stock pot over medium heat with enough canola oil to completely cover the bottom. Add the barley and stir constantly until lightly toasted. Add half of the chicken stock, and stir until well absorbed. Add the other half of the chicken stock, salt, pepper, and liquid smoke (if you didn't smoke the barley), and continue to stir until once again absorbed. Once all the liquid is absorbed, remove from heat and fold in the Parmesan cheese. Garnish with minced chives if desired.

Preheat oven to 350°F.

Bring a cast-iron (or nonstick) pan over medium-high heat with 2 tablespoons canola oil. Remove the grouse from the brine and rinse with cold water. Pat dry with paper towel, then season the marinated grouse breasts with salt and pepper and place the breasts skin-side down in the pan. Bring to medium heat and let cook for 2 minutes. Remove from heat and place in the pre-heated oven for 7 minutes. Remove from the oven and pan, and allow to rest for 5 minutes before slicing.

To plate, arrange the Smoked Barley Risotto and grouse on a serving dish and drizzle with the Cranberry Gastrique.

Adapted from the recipe by Chef Derek Bugge.

WINE SUGGESTION:

Duckhorn Vineyards Napa Valley Merlot

A classic expression of Napa Valley Merlot, this wine offers alluring aromas of lush cherry, raspberry, cocoa, and freshly baked pie crust. The cherry and raspberry notes are echoed on the silky palate where fine-grained tannins and flavors of ripe plum, blueberry, licorice, and subtle baking spice draw the wine to a long, elegant finish.

ONE-PAN OVEN-ROASTED GROUSE

SERVES 2

3 pounds marble potatoes

1 large yellow onion, peeled and large chopped

2 celery stalks, large chopped

2 large carrots, peeled and large chopped

2 teaspoons fresh thyme leaves, divided

Salt and freshly cracked black pepper, to taste

Canola oil, as needed

½ cup chicken stock

1 whole grouse, cleaned

Preheat oven to 350°F.

In a large bowl, add the potatoes, onions, celery, and carrots. Gently toss with 1 teaspoon thyme, along with salt and pepper to taste and a drizzle of canola oil. Toss well to coat. Place the tossed vegetables in a roasting pan. Pour over the chicken stock, then cover loosely with a sheet of aluminum foil. (Note: If the foil is too loose, the vegetables will burn; too tight and the vegetables won't roast.) Place the roasting pan on the middle rack of the oven, and roast for 20 minutes.

Pat the grouse dry with paper towel, and lightly coat the grouse with some canola oil. Season the grouse with salt and pepper, and the remaining thyme. Let rest at room temperature for 20 minutes.

After 20 minutes, remove the pan of vegetables from the oven. Remove the foil and place the seasoned grouse on top of vegetables. Cover with the foil and return the pan to the oven for another 20 minutes.

After 20 minutes, remove the aluminum foil, and continue to roast for another 10 to 12 minutes to add color to the skin. (Note: Watch closely, as it may take a little more time, or a little less, depending on your oven.) Remove the pan from the oven and let rest for 5 minutes before slicing.

Optional: If you are feeling ambitious, you can add the liquid from the roasting pan (about 1 cup) to a saucepan and make your own gravy. Simply whisk with 2 tablespoons butter and 2 tablespoons flour.

Adapted from the recipe by Chef Derek Bugge.

WINE SUGGESTION:

Duckhorn Vineyards Napa Valley Merlot Three Palms Vineyard

Once again, the revered Three Palms Vineyard has yielded a benchmark expression of New World Merlot, with a complex, age-worthy structure, silken tannins, and radiant fruit. On the nose, aromas of huckleberry, plum, Bing cherry, cinnamon, and rose petals are underscored by hints of cocoa and sweet French oak. As it evolves in the glass, flavors of cardamom, cranberry, blueberry, and figs are revealed, as well as elements of earthy minerality that add drama to the long, complex finish.

SMOKED GROUSE

SERVES 2

All-purpose brine (¼ cup kosher salt, ¼ cup sugar, 2 cups water)

1 whole grouse, cleaned

1 tablespoon salt

1 tablespoon freshly cracked black pepper

Smoker with desired chips (apple, alder, or cherry for game birds)

WINE SUGGESTION:

Duckhorn Vineyards Napa Valley Cabernet Sauvignon

A classic expression of Napa Valley Cabernet, this wine combines beautiful complexity with rich intensity. Layers of blackberry, huckleberry, and black currants are supported by firm, dusty tannins that frame the fruit. On the palate, it is juicy and bright, with luxurious cassis and dark berry flavors supported by notes of fig, cardamom, clove, and cracked black pepper that linger on the long, well-structured finish.

Begin by making the brine. In a saucepot over high heat, add the salt, sugar, and water. Bring to a boil then boil for 5 minutes. Remove from heat and chill in the refrigerator. Once the brine is completely cool, arrange the grouse breasts in a baking dish and pour the brine over the top of the breasts. Let marinate in the refrigerator for at least 4 hours, but no more than 8 hours or the grouse will be too salty.

Remove the grouse from the brine and rinse under cold water. Pat dry with paper towel then lightly coat with some canola oil and season with salt and pepper. Note: Experiment with aromatics and citrus like rosemary and lime to infuse more flavor into the grouse.

Preheat an outdoor smoker to 200°F.

Place the grouse on the middle rack, and smoke for 30 minutes. After 30 minutes, remove the grouse from the smoker and wrap in aluminum foil. Note: If you want to finish in the smoker, keep the grouse wrapped in aluminum foil as you would a brisket, and continue to smoke until the internal temperature of the grouse has reached 155°F.

Otherwise, preheat the oven to 350°F.

Place the wrapped grouse on the middle rack and roast for 20 minutes. Note: Ensure the internal temperature of the grouse has reached 155°F. If not, place back in the oven, unwrapped, and continue to roast until the temperature is reached. Remove the grouse from the oven and let rest for 5 minutes before slicing.

Adapted from the recipe by Chef Derek Bugge.

HUNGARIAN PARTRIDGE

Perdix perdix

Hungarian Partridge (a.k.a. Huns, Gray Partridge, and English Partridge) were introduced to the United States from Europe in the late 1700s. The birds populated successfully throughout the prairie states of Washington, Oregon, Idaho, Montana, Wyoming, Montana, Nevada, Nebraska, North and South Dakota, Iowa, Wisconsin, and Minnesota.

The Hungarian Partridge and the chukar partridge are birds of a feather, so to speak. The primary difference between them is the type of terrain each bird is found in. The Hungarian partridge is a popular upland game bird throughout the plains of North America, and a healthy, stable population of Huns resides in the north central part of the United States. Hungarian partridges are a non-migratory game bird.

The Hungarian partridge is a plump-sized game bird with a stubby neck, and it is about 11 to 13 inches long. Huns weigh slightly less than a pound. Both sexes look similar. Huns prefer living in wide-open areas. Grasslands, crop fields of hay or grains, hedgerows, draws, ditches, and some riparian cover are all prime habitats for huns. They mostly forage on waste grains (grains left on the ground after harvest), wild fruits, grass, seeds, insects, and alfalfa.

When alarmed, particularly when they are in open areas, huns generally run first instead of flying away. When they're flushed from cover, though, a covey of birds will explode squawking loudly as they quickly fly away—momentarily confusing hunters with which bird to shoot.

Huns are homebodies. When flushed from a patch of cover, they return to the same spot within a short period of time. Hunting Hungarian partridge requires a lot of walking, but mostly over open negotiable terrain. If a covey is hidden in heavy cover, approach the spot slowly and have the shotgun at the ready, as huns will hold tight in thick brush. The bird's behavior provides hunters ample opportunity to get set before they flush. The ideal shotgun for hunting Huns is a 12-gauge shotgun with #7½ shot loads.

Huns are a superb upland bird to eat. Like other game birds, it is best to eviscerate each hun before placing it in a game bag. Removing the entrails and wiping the chest cavity free of blood will let the meat drain and cool more quickly, thereby enhancing the flavor of the meat tenfold. Once back at the vehicle, place the cleaned birds in an ice-filled portable cooler to increase the overall taste and tenderness of the meat. Because their skin is a little stronger than some other game birds, plucking Huns is quicker and easier. Plucking a game bird presents the opportunity to grill a bird on a spit or roast in an oven.

Huns can be prepared in many of the same ways that other smaller upland birds like doves, woodcock, quail, snipe, and chukar are cooked. All the recipes for these smaller upland birds are basically interchangeable. What sets them apart, however, is the use of a variety of different sauces, spices, and cooking methods. Hun meat is mild and is *slightly* whiter than other similarly sized upland birds.

Huns, like other small upland birds, can be cooked whole, in quarters or deboned. It can be baked, grilled, smoked, roasted (with brandy or wine), braised, boiled, put in a casserole, slow cooker, or even made into chili. No matter how Hun is cooked, as long as it is not overcooked, it will be a superb wild-game upland bird eating experience. Generally, two birds will provide enough for one adult to eat.

CHUKAR PARTRIDGE

Alectoris chukar

The Chukar Partridge (a.k.a. Chukar, Devil Birds, and Red Legs) were introduced to the western United States in the 1920s. Chukar are found in several states including California, Washington, Arizona, Colorado, Idaho, Nevada, Utah, Wyoming, South Dakota, New Hampshire, Connecticut, New Jersey, and even as far away as Hawaii.

Chukars are stout birds that generally weigh slightly over one pound and measure about 13 to 14 inches long. They have a gray breast, light brown back, and bright red beaks. Chukars prefer drier habitat where they feed on leaves, wild fruits, seeds, insects, and grasses. They prefer rocky hillsides filled with a lot of scrub growth (that pinches and sticks both hunter and dog). Chukars are a skittish bird. When flushed, like its cousin the Hun, chukars run first and fly later. When they take to the air, though, they are very strong and fast fliers. However, unlike the Hun, chukars will only fly off for short distances.

There's a popular adage about hunting chukar that clearly defines what hunting these birds is all about: *The first time you hunt chukar, it's for fun. Every time after, it's for revenge!* This game bird is *totally* prepared to turn a hunt into a scenic walk for even the most die-hard, experienced upland game hunter. A majority of chukar hunts don't end with a full game bag. Although some hunters use a 12-gauge for hunting chukars, an ideal choice is a 16- or 20-gauge shotgun loaded with high brass #6 shot.

Upland hunters generally rank the flavor of chukars as one of the top three upland game birds. With the appropriate field care, chukar is quite tasty. The meat is white, firm, and tender. It has a distinct flavor all its own and doesn't taste like chicken! Chukar can be made in all the same ways mentioned above to prepare Huns.

ROAST PARTRIDGE WITH SAGE, THYME & CIDER

SERVES 2

2 whole partridges, cleaned

Salt and freshly cracked black
pepper, as needed

1 bunch fresh sage

1 bunch fresh thyme sprigs

1 garlic bulb, halved

1 tablespoon olive oil

2 tablespoons butter

3½ ounces apple cider

5 ounces heavy cream

1 teaspoon Dijon mustard

Preheat the oven to 400°F.

Season the partridges with salt and pepper and place in a small roasting tray. Next, tuck the sage and thyme in and around the birds. Add the two halves of the garlic bulb then drizzle the olive oil over the partridges. Place one tablespoon of butter on top of each partridge, then place the roasting tray in the oven.

Roast the partridges for 20 to 25 minutes, or until the skin is golden-brown.

Remove the roasting tray from the oven and remove the partridges to a clean plate, positioning them upside down and leaving them to rest somewhere warm. Meanwhile, place the roasting tray directly over medium heat. Make the sauce by adding the apple cider and bringing the contents of the tray to a boil. Add the cream and stir in the mustard. Bring the sauce back to a boil, then lower the heat and simmer gently for about 5 minutes, until nicely reduced and beginning to thicken. Season the sauce with salt and pepper.

Return the partridges to the roasting tray along with any juices left on the plate. Bring to the table in the tray, then place one partridge on each plate and spoon plenty of sauce over each bird.

Adapted from the recipe by Gather: Simple, Seasonal Recipes from Gill Meller, *head chef at River Cottage.*

WINE SUGGESTION:

Duckhorn Vineyards Napa Valley Merlot

A classic expression of Napa Valley Merlot, this wine offers alluring aromas of lush cherry, raspberry, cocoa, and freshly baked pie crust. The cherry and raspberry notes are echoed on the silky palate, where fine-grained tannins and flavors of ripe plum, blueberry, licorice, and subtle baking spice draw the wine to a long, elegant finish.

PARTRIDGE BREAST ON BLACK PUDDING WITH RED WINE AND CRANBERRY REDUCTION

SERVES 2

1 cup red wine

2 teaspoons whole berry
cranberry sauce

1 tablespoon vegetable oil

2 tablespoons butter

2 slices black pudding

2 partridge breast fillets,
cleaned

Salt and freshly cracked black
pepper

Fresh chopped sage, as needed,
for garnish

In a small saucepan over low heat, add the wine and cranberry sauce. Bring to a simmer, then reduce by half. Stir frequently. Remove from heat and set aside.

Preheat two small pans over medium heat. Add the oil to one, and the butter to the other. Add the black pudding to the pan with the oil and fry for 4 minutes on each side. While the black pudding is cooking, season the partridge breasts with salt and pepper, and add to the pan with the butter. Sear for 2 minutes on each side, then remove from heat and cover with foil (note: the partridge will continue to cook). Remove the black pudding from the heat and set aside.

To plate, gently pour the red wine and cranberry reduction to cover the base of a deep serving plate. Place the two slices of bread pudding in the center of the reduction sauce. Slide the partridge breasts in half and arrange on top of the black pudding. Garnish with fresh sage just before serving.

Adapted from the recipe by Gordon Hamilton and Delishably.com.

WINE SUGGESTION:

Duckhorn Vineyards Napa Valley Howell Mountain Cabernet Sauvignon

Howell Mountain is rightfully legendary for the character and quality of its mountain-grown Cabernet Sauvignon, and this wine shows why. On the nose, robust aromas of currant and blackberry mingle with undercurrents of sweet baking spices, tea leaf, cocoa, and clove. Dusty tannins frame the rich dark berry fruit, with savory undertones providing a depth and complexity that carries through to a long, robust finish.

POT-ROASTED PARTRIDGE
WITH RED CABBAGE, GARLIC & JUNIPER

SERVES 4

2 tablespoons olive oil

Salt and freshly cracked black
  pepper

4 whole partridges, cleaned

1 (4½-ounce) package pancetta,
  cubed

2 medium-sized onions, finely
  sliced

1 garlic clove, peeled and
  crushed

6 juniper berries, lightly
  crushed

1 pound red cabbage, finely
  shredded (core and outer
  leaves removed)

2 level tablespoons light brown
  sugar

1¼ cups red wine

Small cooked red potatoes, if
  desired

Cranberry jelly, if desired

Place a Dutch oven over medium-high heat. Add the olive oil. While oil is heating, season the partridges with the salt and pepper. Place the birds in the Dutch oven and brown them evenly on all sides. Remove the partridges and set aside. Next, add the pancetta and cook until browned, about 4 or 5 minutes. Remove and set aside. Add the onions and sauté until softened, about 5 minutes. Then add the garlic and juniper berries. Stir and cook for 1 minute. Next, add the cabbage, and allow to cook for about 15 minutes, stirring occasionally.

Preheat the oven to 350°F.

Add the sugar, red wine, and browned pancetta to the Dutch oven, and season with salt and pepper. Stir well, then place the partridges on their backs on top of the cabbage and bring to a simmer. Cover and place in the oven. Roast for 40 minutes. Then remove the lid and let everything cook for another 10 minutes or so to crisp up the skin of the birds.

To serve, plate one partridge per person on a bed of red cabbage, with some cranberry jelly as an accompaniment and perhaps some small red potatoes.

Adapted from the recipe by Gordon Hamilton and Deliaonline.com.

WINE SUGGESTION:

Duckhorn Vineyards Napa Valley Cabernet Sauvignon

A classic expression of Napa Valley Cabernet, this wine combines beautiful complexity with rich intensity. Layers of blackberry, huckleberry, and black currants are supported by firm, dusty tannins that frame the fruit. On the palate, it is juicy and bright, with luxurious cassis and dark berry flavors supported by notes of fig, cardamom, clove, and cracked black pepper that linger on the long, well-structured finish.

RING-NECKED PHEASANT

Phasianus colchicus

Pheasants (a.k.a. Ringnecks, roosters, longtails, longspurs, and ditch-chickens) are part of the categorization known as "upland game birds," which are birds that are hunted with bird dogs. Ringnecks were imported from Shanghai, China, and introduced into Oregon in 1881. They quickly took over the top spot of America's most quintessential and most popular upland game bird. They are truly considered as All American as apple pie.

It didn't take the Ringneck long to thrive in its new home and, within a few short decades, Ringnecks were found inhabiting lands from coast to coast. As any upland hunter will attest, the Ring-necked pheasant is acclaimed for being the most favorite hunted upland bird in the United States.

Males are vibrantly colored with iridescent feathers and a bright white neck collar. But captive breeding and crossbreeding of pheasants has accounted for many atypical color variations as well. A mature pheasant cock bird is 30 to 36 inches long, including its tail. Adult males weigh about three pounds. Males make high-pitched rooster-like squawking sounds and can be heard from up to a mile away.

Pheasants get most of their food from the ground by scratching or digging with their beaks. Ring-necked pheasants eat seeds, especially grains, grasses, buds, leaves, roots, wild fruits and nuts, and insects. They forage in grasslands, hayfields, fruit orchards, woodland edges, and brushy shrubs, and sometimes pick grains from cow manure in pastures. Ring-necked pheasants can also inhabit an impressive range of habitats: In Hawaii, pheasants are found from sea level up to 11,000 feet. They can also live in forests, grasslands, and deserts.

Ringnecks have specialized, formidable breast muscles. The muscles supply powerful bursts of flight, allowing pheasants to rapidly escape a predator. Pheasants can flush from cover at nearly a vertical angle from a standing position and swiftly attain speeds of nearly 40 miles per hour.

Because they are usually found in tall vegetation and old fields, Ringnecks can be hard to see while hunting. Fortunately, good bird dogs smell them long before they see the birds, alerting hunters to a possible upcoming flushing pheasant. Hunters also need to keep a sharp eye out for pheasants running along the ground between patches of cover. A seasoned old cock-bird has learned it is sometimes better to escape on the ground than flushing into the air.

Late fall and early winter are good times to hunt Ring-necked pheasants. Harvested crops like corn and soybeans are highly attractive to pheasants during these times. Other good places to hunt Ring-necked pheasants are in old abandoned fields and fruit orchards. Pheasants also hole up in grass ditches, hedges, marshes, woodland borders, and brushy groves.

Hunting these birds with a good bird dog can prove to be a top-notch way of covering fields, brush, and other areas where pheasants hang tight. Because of the amazing speed they reach when flushing and flying, it is recommended that hunters aim at the forward third of the bird to avoid hitting its long tail. In thick cover, a 20-gauge equipped with a modified choke is a terrific choice. In more open areas and farm fields, a 12-gauge is a better choice.

Today, the top best pheasant-hunting states, in order of preference, are South Dakota (*the ultimate pheasant hunting location*), Montana, Minnesota, North Dakota, Nebraska, Iowa, Kansas, and eastern Colorado. Pheasant hunters can't go wrong in these states. However, Ring-necked pheasants can be hunted across the country on shooting preserves, private lands, lodges, and public lands where game agencies stock Ringnecks. No matter where a bird hunter chooses to stalk pheasants, they are assured of an exciting hunting experience, especially when experiencing the thrill of watching pheasant dogs "work."

Since the early settlers hung pheasants out to "age," there isn't a bird hunter today who doesn't prize preparing a meal of pheasant meat. Many hunters and non-hunters say, "It tastes like chicken," and, in some cases, it does. Prepared well, pheasant meat can taste better than chicken but not as good as quail.

Most times, pheasant meat is darker than chicken meat, and this is particularly the case when hunting wild pheasants. If the bird was farm-raised or was cross-bred, the pheasant meat has a lighter pinkish color like chicken. The bottom line about *wild* pheasant meat is an old bird can be tough. Like all wild game, what they eat is absorbed into their systems, producing different flavors of the meat. The same is true for pheasant meat, it definitely is influenced by what the bird eats. Young wild birds, particularly hens, generally taste better than old cock birds. Birds shot on hunting preserves eat better food; therefore, they taste much better than wild birds. Pheasants prepared in fine-dining establishments are almost guaranteed to be farm-raised, assuring for a top-notch, mouth-watering dish. With all that said, though, pheasant meat cooked properly and seasoned appropriately will provide a wonderful meal.

PHEASANT WITH SAUERKRAUT

SERVES 4–6

4 thick-cut slices bacon, diced

2 (2-pound) pheasants, skinned
  and cut into serving pieces
  including backs

2 pounds fresh (not canned)
  sauerkraut, drained and
  rinsed

1½ cups dry white wine

1 teaspoon juniper berries

2 teaspoons chopped fresh
  rosemary, dried thyme, or
  1 fresh sprig of either

2 whole cloves

1 large bay leaf

Chicken stock

Salt and freshly ground black
  pepper to taste

Preheat the oven to 300°F.

In a large Dutch oven, sauté the bacon over medium heat until crisp, about 5 minutes. Add the legs, backs, and wings, and brown in batches on all sides, 3 to 4 minutes. (Refrigerate the breast pieces, covered, until needed.) Add to the Dutch oven the sauerkraut, wine, juniper berries, rosemary, cloves, and bay leaf. Cook over medium heat until about half the liquid has evaporated, about 10 to 15 minutes. Place the Dutch oven in the oven, uncovered. Bake for about 2 hours, stirring occasionally and adding stock as needed, until the legs are tender and the sauerkraut is slightly browned.

Remove the Dutch oven from the oven, discard the backs, wings, and bay leaf, season to taste, cover, and keep warm.

Raise the oven temperature to 425°F. Salt and pepper the pheasant breasts, and place them on a rack in a roasting pan. Roast for 20 minutes, or until the juices run clear when they are pierced with a fork. Remove the breasts from the roasting pan, set aside, and keep warm. Briefly reheat the legs in the Dutch oven. Slice the meat from the breasts and arrange attractively with the legs and sauerkraut.

Adapted from the recipe by Chef John Ash and James O. Fraioli from the cookbook Wild.

WINE SUGGESTION:

2018 King Estate "Estate Grown" Willamette Valley Gewürztraminer

Gewürztraminer is an aromatic grape varietal that thrives in cool climate conditions. These conditions are perfectly suited for the small parcels of Gewürztraminer found on block 19 of King Estate Vineyard, one of the coolest and highest elevation sites in Oregon.

WINE SUGGESTION:

2018 King Estate Four Nobles "Estate Grown" Willamette Valley Cuvée Blanc

In the Grand Cru vineyards of Alsace, the French government requires that wines be made from the "Noble Grapes": Pinot Gris, Riesling, Muscat, and Gewürztraminer. These varietals, known for making aromatic, crisp, and dry white wines, are planted on the estate vineyard in Lorane, Oregon. King Estate's cool climate creates perfect growing conditions for these Four Noble grapes and pays tribute to the beautiful wines of Alsace.

KUNG PAO PHEASANT

SERVES 2

2 boneless, skinless pheasant
 breasts, about ⅔ pound
2 tablespoons peanut oil
6 or more small dried red chilies
 preferably Sichuanese, snipped
 in half, seeds discarded
1 teaspoon whole Sichuan pepper
1 tablespoon peeled and thinly
 sliced ginger
2 medium cloves garlic, thinly
 sliced
4 scallions thinly sliced on the bias,
 white part only
⅔ cup roasted unsalted peanuts

Marinade

½ teaspoon salt
2 teaspoons light soy sauce
1 teaspoon Shaoxing rice wine or
 medium-dry sherry
1½ teaspoons potato flour or 2¼
 teaspoons cornstarch
1 tablespoon water

Sauce

3 teaspoons sugar
1 teaspoon cornstarch
1 teaspoon dark soy sauce
1 teaspoon light soy sauce
1 tablespoon black Chinese vinegar
 or balsamic vinegar
1 teaspoon sesame oil
1 tablespoon chicken stock or water

Cut the pheasant as evenly as possible into ½-inch strips, and then cut into small cubes. Place in a small bowl and mix in all of the marinade ingredients.

In a small bowl, combine the sugar, cornstarch, soy sauces, vinegar, sesame oil, and chicken stock or water to make the sauce. Set aside.

Add 2 tablespoons of the oil to a wok or skillet, and heat over a high flame. When the oil is hot, but not yet smoking, add the chilies and Sichuan pepper, and stir-fry briefly (10 seconds) until the peppers are crisp and the oil is spicy and fragrant. Take care not to burn the spices. Remove the wok from the heat if necessary to prevent overheating.

Quickly add the pheasant, and fry over a high flame, stirring constantly. As soon as the pheasant cubes have separated, add the ginger, garlic, and scallions, and continue to stir-fry for a few minutes until they are fragrant and the meat is cooked through (test one of the larger pieces to make sure).

Give the sauce a stir and add it to the wok, continuing to stir and toss. As soon as the sauce is thick and shiny, stir in the peanuts, and serve immediately.

Adapted from the recipe by Chef John Ash and James O. Fraioli from the cookbook Wild.

ROAST PHEASANT STUFFED WITH WILD RICE

SERVES 2–4

1½ cups cooked wild rice

2 tablespoons butter

1½ cups finely chopped onion

½ cup finely chopped celery

2 teaspoons finely chopped
garlic

Salt and freshly ground black
pepper

1 ounce dried porcini
mushrooms, soaked in warm
water for 30 minutes, drained,
and chopped

¾ cup sliced cremini mushrooms

⅓ cup chicken stock

¼ cup dry white wine

½ cup golden raisins

¼ cup chopped fresh flat-leaf
parsley

1 tablespoon chopped fresh
thyme or 1 teaspoon dried
thyme

1 (2½-pound or so) whole
pheasant

In a medium saucepan, bring 4½ cups water to a boil over high heat. Add the rice and return to boil. Cover, reduce the heat to a simmer, and cook until the rice is tender, 40 to 50 minutes. Drain the rice and set aside to cool.

Meanwhile, in a large heavy skillet, melt the butter over medium heat. Add the onions, celery, and garlic. Season lightly with salt and pepper to taste, and cook, stirring, until the onions just begin to brown. Add the mushrooms and cook until all the liquid released from the mushrooms has evaporated, about 5 minutes. Add the stock and wine and stir, scraping the bottom of the pan to incorporate any browned bits. Cook until most of the liquid is evaporated. Set aside.

Preheat the oven to 425°F.

Transfer the cooled rice to a bowl and stir in the reserved cooked vegetables along with the raisins, parsley, and thyme. Season with salt and pepper to taste.

Season the pheasant inside and out with salt and pepper. Stuff the cavity loosely with the rice mixture, then arrange on a rack set in a roasting pan. Place in the oven and roast for 10 minutes, then reduce the oven temperature to 350°F and roast until the juices in the thigh run clear when pierced with a knife (or use an instant-read thermometer inserted into the thickest part of the thigh until internal temperature reaches 160°F), about 40 minutes. Let the pheasant rest for 5 minutes before carving.

Adapted from the recipe by Chef John Ash and James O. Fraioli from the cookbook Wild.

WHITE-TAILED PTARMIGAN

Lagopus leucura

White-tailed ptarmigan (a.k.a. snow quail) are another subspecies within the numerous families of grouse. One noticeable difference of ptarmigan as compared to all other grouse is that the tops and bottoms of their toes are covered with stiff feathers.

Ptarmigans are widely distributed throughout Canada, where they are the official bird of the province Newfoundland and Labrador. In the United States, three kinds of ptarmigan are found in Alaska where the ptarmigan is the official state bird. The three species include: the willow, rock, and white-tailed ptarmigans. All three species are found mostly in Denali, Alaska. In the lower forty-eight states, there are isolated populations of only white-tailed ptarmigan. They are an alpine species found in the highest northern ranges of the Rocky Mountains above the timberline in Montana, Colorado, New Mexico, and the Cascade Mountains of Washington. White-tailed ptarmigan are very resilient grouse, capable of enduring harsh terrains and cold inclement weather.

All three species of ptarmigan can be hunted and prepared almost identically. Only the size of each bird is different. The smallest ptarmigan is the white-tailed ptarmigan, measuring about 12 inches, and this species is the most accessible ptarmigan for hunters in the continental United States. The Rock ptarmigan is slightly larger at about 14 inches, and the Willow ptarmigan is the largest, measuring about 15 inches. Adults are stocky birds that weigh a little over 1 pound.

For the hardy hunters who stalk ptarmigan at extreme altitudes, in the dead of winter, on snow-shoes, during frigid conditions—the hunt can be arduous at best. If the hunter is not in tip-top shape, the hunt can be downright dangerous. Being physically fit is *the* number one factor in being successful at pursuing alpine white-tailed (and coming home alive). During the fall and winter seasons, hunters can locate snow quail by knowing what food stuffs they are eating that time of year. A white-tailed ptarmigan's diet in autumn includes lichens, berries, willows, catkins, mountain flowers, leaves, and insects when they come across them. In winter, they feed mostly on seeds, alder, twigs, and buds. Locating food sources will put the hunter where the ptarmigans are.

Fortunately, because all three species of ptarmigan live in remote alpine areas, they rarely see humans. This, in turn, makes them somewhat easy targets for the hunter who can shoot straight. In fact, it has been said that in remote areas even a well-placed rock can yield a delicious ptarmigan. Not everyone can put this all together when it's hard to breathe at 12,000 feet, in snow or on steep, rocky hillsides, with blowing frigid winds. Top that with a well-camouflaged bird that often isn't spotted until a covey is flushed. Once a covey is located, however, hunters usually fill their limits quickly. Then it's time to head down the mountain for a bowl of soup, some buttered bread, and a hot meal of ptarmigan.

The recommended gear for hunting light-boned ptarmigan is the lighter shotguns. A 20- or 28-gauge shotgun works well and even a .410 shotgun. Remember that much hunting is done in rugged terrain, so keep your gear as light as possible. If you're hunting early in the season and have the opportunity to take younger birds, 7½, 8, and even 9 shot will work. Later on in the season, as the birds feather out and get larger, hunters tend to use a larger shot like No 6. The heavier shot also will go a bit farther, as the more mature birds fly faster than the younger ones earlier in the season. If the terrain you're in is thick cover for close shots, use a modified or improved-cylinder choke. For the more open areas, full chokes will do.

Ptarmigan meat is red and dense. It must be prepared well to please the palate. Be sure not to overcook it and have the right type of wine that highlights a red game meat.

>>>

WINE SUGGESTION:

2018 King Estate Quail Run & Gold Vineyard Rogue Valley Roussanne-Marsanne

The history of this classic blend of Roussanne and Marsanne is rooted in France's Rhone Valley. King Estate's blend comes from the warm climate of Oregon's Rogue Valley. This rich and succulent wine is unique in its ability to showcase delicate flavors such as apricot and honeysuckle, yet it retains a full-bodied roundness that is complemented by balanced oak.

PTARMIGAN KABOBS

SERVES 4–6

4 ptarmigan breasts
Teriyaki sauce, as needed
Fresh jalapeños, as needed
Fresh pineapple slices, as
    needed
Bacon slices, as needed
Cream cheese, as needed
Salt and pepper
1 green bell pepper, seeded,
    cored, and cut into chunks
1 red bell pepper, seeded, cored,
    and cut into chunks
1 yellow onion, peeled and
    sliced into chunks

Remove the breast meat from the bone of each ptarmigan so you have each breast (and breast tenderloin) separate and free of bones. Next, split each breast in half, making it a thinner piece of meat. This not only makes it easier for wrapping but also takes less time to cook. Rinse the meat to ensure there aren't any remaining feathers or shot in the meat, then pat dry with a paper towel.

Transfer the breast meat to a bowl or large ziptop bag and cover with teriyaki sauce. Marinate overnight.

When ready to cook, remove the meat from the refrigerator and soak 4 to 6 wooden skewers in water for at least 30 minutes prior to grilling. Preheat the grill to 325°F.

Prepare the kabobs by slicing the jalapeños either in half or in quarters depending on your taste. Slice the pineapple into ½-inch to 1-inch slices. Finally, cut the bacon strips in half.

Next, lay the marinated breast meat on a clean counter. Add a piece of jalapeño, some cream cheese, and a pineapple slice onto each piece of meat. Then roll up and wrap with a piece of bacon. Continue with the remaining pieces of breast meat. Season with salt and pepper.

Skewer the wrapped ptarmigan pieces onto the wooden skewers while alternating with pieces of green and red bell pepper and slices of sweet yellow onion.

Place skewers on the preheated grill, and grill until charred and the internal temperature of the meat reaches 140 to 145°F. Remove from grill and let rest for several minutes before serving.

Adapted from the recipe by The Alaska Life.

BRAISED PTARMIGAN

SERVES 8

8 ptarmigans, cleaned
Salt and fresh cracked black
   pepper
6 tablespoons butter, divided
Warm water, as needed
6 juniper berries, roughly
   crushed
1¼ cups heavy cream
1 tablespoon red currant jelly
1 tablespoon all-purpose flour
Red cabbage, optional
Caramelized potatoes, optional

Rub the ptarmigans inside and out with salt and freshly ground black pepper.

Melt 3 tablespoons of butter in a Dutch oven and, in batches, brown the ptarmigans on all sides. Next, pour enough lukewarm water to half-cover the birds. Add the juniper berries, cover, and simmer for 20 minutes. Add the cream, cover, and simmer for 1 hour, or until the birds are tender.

Remove the birds from the broth and keep warm. Strain the juices through a sieve and return to a clean pan. Whisk the red currant jelly and flour into the sauce until slightly thickened. Whisk in the remaining 3 tablespoons butter. Adjust the seasoning if necessary.

Remove the breast meat and legs from the ptarmigan carcasses. Serve with the sauce spooned over the top along with sides likes red cabbage and caramelized potatoes.

Adapted from the recipe by Waitrose.com

WINE SUGGESTION:

2014 King Estate 25th Anniversary Willamette Valley Pinot Noir

King Estate's 25th Anniversary Pinot Noir is made from other vineyards that this vineyard has worked with from very early on. A vivid ruby color foretells lush flavors of ripe raspberry, leather, dried tobacco leaves, cinnamon, and mushroom. The palate is expressive with red cherries, violets, clove, and vanilla. The mid-palate shows off the depth that Willamette Valley Pinot Noir is famed for—balanced acidity, fine tannins, and ripe fruit all flow together in perfect unison to create a long and opulent finish.

HOMEMADE PTARMIGAN STEW

SERVES 12

4 tablespoons extra virgin olive oil, divided

1½ large red onions, peeled and diced

3 large cloves garlic, peeled and crushed

5 ptarmigan breasts

2 grouse breasts (or more ptarmigan or other small game bird)

4 tablespoons flour

1 teaspoon salt

1 teaspoon black pepper

6 cups white potatoes, chopped, skin-on

3 cups diced sweet potatoes

3 cups diced carrots

1 cup fresh or frozen green peas

5 cups (or 2 large cartons) low-sodium chicken stock

1 (14-ounce) can diced tomatoes

2 bay leaves

1 teaspoon celery seed or 3 stalks fresh celery

1 teaspoon poultry seasoning

¼ teaspoon crushed red pepper or cayenne pepper

2 tablespoons dried crushed rosemary

½ teaspoon cinnamon

1 tablespoon apple cider vinegar

In a large stock pot or Dutch oven over medium heat, add 2 tablespoons of the olive oil. When hot, add the onions and garlic and, stirring often, sauté until soft, about 5 minutes. While the onions and garlic are cooking, add the bird breasts to a large bowl and add the flour, salt, and pepper. Toss well to coat. Add the meat to the pot, along with the remaining 2 tablespoons of olive oil and brown the breasts on all sides. Then add the potatoes, sweet potatoes, carrots, peas, chicken stock, diced tomatoes, bay leaves, celery, poultry seasoning, red pepper, rosemary, cinnamon, and the vinegar. Stir well to combine. Then reduce heat to low and let simmer, stirring occasionally, for 1½ hours, or until the breast meat is tender and falls apart easily. Remove from heat, remove bay leaves, and serve.

Adapted from the recipe by Sarita Harbour and An Off Grid Life.

WINE SUGGESTION:

2017 King Estate Domaine "Estate Grown" Willamette Valley Pinot Noir

King Estate Domaine Pinot Gris is made from the highest quality, certified Biodynamic and organic grapes sourced exclusively from King Estate in Oregon's beautiful Willamette Valley. The estate vineyard is one of the coolest sites in the valley, sitting between 800 and 1,200 feet in elevation. This bottle represents the King family's commitment to sustainable agricultural practices and artisan winemaking methods.

QUAIL

Ondontophoridae

There are six native species of quail in the United States. Quail are found in a variety of habitats from mountain ranges to deserts. The species of quail that inhabit the United States include the Bobwhite, California, Mountain, Scaled, Mearn's, and Gambel's quail.

BOBWHITE QUAIL

Colinus virginianus

Bobwhite Quail are more correctly called the Northern Bobwhite Quail. It is the most common and recognizable of all six species of quail. In fact, Bobwhite quail are the number two upland game bird in the United States and have the largest range of any game bird in America. Bobwhites are also known as Northern Bobwhites, whistlers, and bobs. Males have a white throat and brow stripe bordered by black compared to brown-colored females. Northern Bobwhites are small birds weighing a mere 6 to 8 ounces and measuring about 10 inches.

Bobwhites are found east of the Rocky Mountains, south of the Great Lakes, throughout the Midwest, and as far north as New England and other eastern states. However, the real center of bobwhite populations and hunting activity takes place in all the southern states in the country. Whistlers are very fond of edge habitats where agricultural lands and native vegetation border one another but generally avoid hardwood forests. They are most abundant in mixed areas of fields, forests, and croplands. Like all game birds, bobwhites eat a wide variety of foods including seeds, grains, fruits, and insects.

CALIFORNIA VALLEY QUAIL (A.K.A. VALLEY QUAIL AND CALIFORNIA QUAIL)

California valley quail are the most popular of the five species of western quail. Valley quail are to the West what bobwhites are to the rest of the country. California valley quail are found from western Washington, south to Baja California, and east into parts of Idaho, Nevada, and Utah.

These small birds are best hunted with lightweight, quick-pointing shotguns. When it comes to hunting quail, there is no need for a 12-gauge shotgun. Most experienced quail hunters agree that a 20-gauge is an ideal gun that makes the most sense. When it comes down to quail-hunting tactics, the three most central elements that can impact how, when, and where to hunt quail are wind, rain, and, the most vital element, a new food source. Anytime a new foodstuff becomes ripe, or there is a freshly harvested grain field, or even the subtle odor of a newly available wild plant, it will draw in quail like the event horizon of a black hole draws in material. Quail will instantly take advantage of any new food item. Quail gunners who recognize this will be able to put up coveys of quail to the gun. Equally important, hunters must know not only where to look for birds, but also the best time of the day to find bevies of quail. When hunters find a flock, go to it straight away. Be prepared for a quick explosive eruption from cover. As soon as the quail get above the height of the surrounding cover, they generally head straight, fast, and low. Gunners only get a brief window of opportunity at these challenging, small, and lightning-quick targets.

Now comes the most important fact about quail. From field to fork, quail are a delectable wild game. It's hard to find a fine-dining restaurant that doesn't offer an entrée of quail. That speaks volumes for how quail meat can please the palate and warm the soul of even the most discerning food connoisseur.

MOUNTAIN QUAIL (A.K.A. PAINTED QUAIL, MOUNTAIN PARTRIDGE, PLUMED QUAIL)

These are found above the valleys and foothills. Mountain quail are easily identified by their large size—up to 12 inches. They are the largest of all other quail species found in the United States. Another distinguishing feature of these quail is their loud, sharp, and mournful whistle. If hunters can mimic this vocalization, the quail will quickly answer, giving away their location.

GAMBEL'S QUAIL (A.K.A. DESERT QUAIL)

Gambel's quail are found in dry regions of the southwestern United States. They are easily recognized by their top knots and scaly plumage on their undersides. They have gray plumage on their bodies, and males have copper feathers on the top of their heads, black faces, and white stripes above their eyes.

SCALED QUAIL (A.K.A. BLUE QUAIL)

Scaled quail are known for their blue-scaled appearance. Along with its scaly markings, the bird is easily identified by its white crest that resembles a tuft of cotton.

MEARN'S QUAIL (A.K.A. MONTEZUMA QUAIL)

Mearn's quail have the smallest range in the United States. They are found in southern Texas, New Mexico, Arizona, and Mexico. Mearn live in mountain areas populated with oak and juniper trees as well as grasslands. They have a unique coloration of feathers that aids in their means of camouflage.

ASIAN-STYLE QUAIL

SERVES 6

2 tablespoons honey garlic barbecue sauce

2 tablespoons sesame seeds

1 tablespoon chili garlic sauce

3 tablespoons sesame oil

2 tablespoons honey

3 cloves garlic, peeled and minced

1 tablespoon fresh ginger, grated

¼ cup white wine

¼ cup soy sauce

6 whole quail, cleaned

2 tablespoons vegetable oil

In a large bowl, add the honey garlic barbecue sauce, sesame seeds, chili garlic sauce, sesame oil, honey, garlic, ginger, white wine, and soy sauce. Mix well to combine. Next, rinse the quail and pat dry thoroughly with paper towels. Add the quail and toss liberally to coat. Cover and refrigerate for at least 30 minutes, turning the quail occasionally.

Preheat the oven to 375°F.

In a large oven-proof skillet or Dutch oven, heat the over medium-high heat. Add the quail, reserving the marinade, and brown evenly on all sides.

Remove the quail and cooking vessel and transfer to the preheated oven. Roast the quail, uncovered, until cooked through, about 20 to 30 minutes. Transfer the quail to a serving platter and drizzle with some of the marinade. Serve immediately.

Adapted from the recipe by Joanna Cismaru and JoCooks.com

WINE SUGGESTION:

2017 King Estate Kennel Vineyard Willamette Valley Chardonnay

Established in 2007, Kennel is nestled in the Willamette Valley, halfway between Corvallis and Monmouth, Oregon. Consisting of 28 acres, Kennel is considered a warm site but benefits from coastal breezes and cool nights. This wine was aged in 30 percent new French oak and underwent malolactic fermentation and *sur lie* aging. The resulting wine is a silky, full-bodied Chardonnay.

SOUTHERN FRIED QUAIL

SERVES 4

8 whole quail, cleaned

Salt and freshly cracked black
  pepper, to taste

All-purpose flour

Peanut oil, as needed

Cheesy grits, optional

Roasted asparagus, optional

Rinse the quail and pat dry thoroughly with paper towels. Season each quail with salt and pepper, inside and out.

In a large bowl, add enough flour to dust each quail. Toss each quail in the flour until coated. Shake off any excess flour. Set aside.

Heat a large cast-iron skillet over high-heat with enough peanut oil to fill one inch of the pan. Add the quails to the hot oil and "deep-fry" until golden-brown on all sides. When done, remove from the oil and let drain on a paper towel–lined plate. Serve hot with cheese grits and roasted asparagus.

Adapted from the recipe by Lana Stuart and Never Enough Thyme.

WINE SUGGESTION:

2017 King Estate Weinbau Vineyard Columbia Valley Cabernet Franc

Located in the Wahluke Slope, sub-AVA of the greater Columbia Valley AVA, Weinbau's south-facing alluvial slope consists of perfectly draining soils. The vineyard experiences moderate temperatures that help elongate hang time with ideal ripening conditions. The microclimate produces a richer, riper style of Cabernet Franc. Flavors include plum, anise, and tobacco leaf.

ROASTED QUAIL

SERVES 2

4 whole quail, cleaned
½ teaspoon salt
½ teaspoon freshly cracked
   black pepper
4 cloves garlic, peeled and
   smashed, divided
1 lemon, quartered, divided
4 tablespoons melted butter
1 tablespoon fresh rosemary,
   stemmed and chopped

Preheat the oven to 400°F.

Rinse the quail and pat dry thoroughly with paper towels. Season each quail with salt and pepper, inside and out. Next, place the garlic and one-quarter lemon inside the cavity of each quail.

Transfer the quail, breast-side down, to a baking dish, and tuck the legs under the breast cavity.

In a small bowl, combine the melted butter and rosemary. Brush liberally over each quail, then roast until the quail are cooked through, about 40 minutes. Remove the quail and let rest for 10 minutes before serving. The quail are great atop cooked wild rice.

Adapted from the recipe by Kelly Bogard and Texas Table Top *and the Texas Farm Bureau.*

WINE SUGGESTION:

2016 King Estate 7 Rows "Estate Grown" Willamette Valley Pinot Noir
This wine was crafted by third-generation King family member Justin King using grapes exclusively from seven rows of a premium clone 115 Pinot Noir vineyard block, 11a, at King Estate. It was fermented using naturally occurring yeast, aged in French oak for 18 months and left unfiltered.

WILD TURKEY

Meleagris gallopavo

Nearly 2.5 million hunters in the United States pursue wild turkey each year, making it the second most hunted game after deer. The wild turkey is often mistakenly thought of as an "upland game bird." But this isn't so, as upland game birds are land birds hunted with bird dogs. The wild turkey is part of the game bird category. There are ten game birds including ducks, geese, wild turkey, pheasants, partridges, grouse, woodcock, snipes, and quail.

The wild turkeys (a.k.a. Longbeards, boss toms, and gobblers) are considered "ground birds," albeit they are strong fliers. Currently there are more than 7 million wild turkeys roaming North America. They inhabit every US state other than Alaska, and a few Canada provinces, parts of Mexico, Guatemala, and Belize. The six wild turkey species include the Eastern, Osceola, Merriam, Rio Grande, Gould, and Ocellated. The Eastern turkey is the most prolific; its range covers half of the United States. Osceola turkeys live in Florida; Rio Grande turkeys inhabit the Great Plains; Merriam turkeys are found throughout the Rockies; Gould turkeys are found in Mexico and the Ocellated variety are found in Guatemala, Belize, and on the Yucatan Peninsula of Mexico. The Ocellated is by far the most beautifully colored and adorned of all the wild turkey species.

All six species of turkey are hunted similarly. Most states have both spring and fall turkey hunting seasons, but check local game laws. The Eastern turkey, because of its sheer numbers and wide distribution, is the most popular to hunt. Spring is the best time to attract a boss gobbler into shotgun range by imitating the sound of a hen. Another effective tactic is to learn where turkeys are traveling throughout the day and set up in an area to ambush the birds as they pass by. During the fall season, turkeys congregate into flocks. One strategy is to break up the flock and then call the scattered birds back using a locater call. Wild turkeys are extremely sensitive to the slightest movement. Hunters must use head-to-toe camo to cloak themselves from being detected by a wary gobbler's eyes. Turkeys are usually hunted with 20- to 12-gauge shotguns with 3- to 3½-inch turkey shot loads. They can also be hunted using crossbows, compound bows, and/or more traditional archery gear (but always check the state's game laws).

There is no doubt that turkey meat can provide nothing less than quality table fare. Thankfully, it doesn't taste like the recurrent theme that claims most wild game: chicken! Yet, it doesn't taste like a plump, store-bought, brand name, Thanksgiving turkey either. Wild turkey has its own unique flavor.

As for tenderness, like any other bird or animal, domestic or wild game, it depends on what types of food the game eats, its age, and many other elements. Be mindful that wild turkey can be easily overcooked if it's not watched carefully. That's why it can be a daunting task to cook a whole wild turkey in the oven, unless it is a young bird.

The legs and thighs are not as succulent and tender, as they do a lot of the work to get the birds from place to place. The breast meat is, however, more flavorful. Most thigh meat, flavorful or not, is better prepared in slow cookers, stews, or soups. Other ways to use wild turkey include barbecuing the thighs, braising or simmering the wing and leg meat, and then pulling it free from the bone to use Mexican carnitas–style. It can also be used for turkey enchiladas. The taste of wild turkey can be mild and can be enormously moist and flavorful when properly cared for from field to table.

>>>

WINE SUGGESTION:

Wagner Vineyards Estate Winery Sparkling Riesling

Bottle-fermented and left with just a slight touch of sweetness, Wagner's bubbly is crowd-pleaser for all occasions, especially when fried food is on the menu. Whether celebrating a special occasion or just welcoming the weekend, spritz up your meal with this unique expression of the Finger Lakes' premier grape.

BUTTERMILK FRIED TURKEY

SERVES 4

1 wild turkey breast half

1 quart buttermilk

2 cups flour

2 tablespoons salt

1 tablespoon freshly ground
pepper

1 tablespoon granulated garlic

1 tablespoon granulated onion

1 teaspoon cayenne pepper
(more if you prefer spicy)

1 teaspoon white pepper

2 teaspoons rubbed sage

Vegetable oil for frying

Tarragon Butter Sauce

2 tablespoons finely chopped
shallots

½ cup dry vermouth or white
wine

½ cup shellfish or chicken stock

1 tablespoon chopped fresh
tarragon leaves

⅓ cup heavy cream

4 tablespoons chilled, unsalted
butter

Salt to taste

Freshly ground white pepper,
or drops of your favorite hot
sauce

Drops of fresh lemon juice

Cut the breast to ½- to ¾-inch-thick cutlets and soak in buttermilk in the refrigerator overnight.

Mix the flour, salt, pepper, granulated garlic, granulated onion, cayenne pepper, white pepper, and sage to make the seasoned flour. Remove the turkey pieces from the buttermilk and place directly into the seasoned flour. Dredge thoroughly and gently shake off any excess. Pan-fry over medium heat in ¼ inch vegetable oil, turning over once after 4 to 5 minutes, or deep fry for 6 minutes at 350°F.

To make the butter sauce, add the shallots, wine, stock, and tarragon to a small deep saucepan, and bring to a boil over high heat. Boil until the liquid is reduced to ⅓ cup or so. Add the cream, and continue to boil until the mixture is again reduced to about ½ cup or has a light sauce consistency. Reduce the heat to low and whisk in 1 tablespoon of the butter until it's completely absorbed. As you whisk, you can move the saucepan back and forth from low heat to no heat; the trick is to melt the butter into a cream sauce without breaking (which is when the butter separates and the sauce turns oily). Repeat with the remaining butter 1 tablespoon at a time. Strain through a fine-mesh strainer into a clean saucepan, and season to taste with salt, pepper, and drops of lemon juice. Keep warm until ready to serve.

Adapted from the recipe by Outdoor Life's Best Wild Turkey recipe from 2012.

ROASTING A WHOLE WILD TURKEY

The best method is to slow roast the turkey after brining for up to 8 hours. Place the prepared, brined bird in a pan breast-side down with no liquid added and cover with foil. Preheat the oven to 275°F. Use a thermometer to check the temperature, as the roasting temperature is critical. Cook by weight as follows (this is just a guide):

8- to 10-pound turkey: cook 3–3½ hours

10- to 14-pound turkey: cook 3½–4 hours

14- to 18-pound turkey: cook 4–4½ hours

Do not continuously check the oven, as this will cool the oven and extend the cooking time. You also won't end up with a browned, crispy-skinned bird, although your bird will be tender and juicy. The turkey is done cooking when the internal temperature, measured with an instant-read meat thermometer at the thickest point of the bird, reaches at least 165°F.

Adapted from the recipe by Chef John Ash and James O. Fraioli from the cookbook Wild.

WINE SUGGESTION:

Wagner Vineyards Estate Winery Fathom 107

Wagner Vineyards is situated on the eastern shore of Seneca Lake, directly east of the deepest point in all of the Finger Lakes. At 640 feet (or 107 fathoms) deep, Seneca Lake's enormous volume of water provides year-round temperature moderation. This ode to an exceptional body of water blends Riesling and Gewürztraminer to produce a complex and food-friendly aromatic white wine that pairs perfectly with the main meat of Thanksgiving.

WILD TURKEY CARNITAS

SERVES 6

2 turkey legs and thighs

1 tablespoon kosher salt

1 tablespoon black peppercorns, cracked

1 tablespoon coriander seed, cracked

2 teaspoons cumin seed

1 tablespoon oregano, preferably Mexican

2 tablespoons brown sugar

1 small cinnamon stick, broken into pieces

3 small dried hot chilies, such as chili de arbol

2 large bay leaves

⅓ cup fresh orange juice

2 tablespoons fresh lime juice

4 tablespoons lard or olive oil

Corn tortillas warmed for serving

Garnishes (use any or all): Finely shredded green cabbage, finely sliced radishes, finely diced white onion, cilantro sprigs, lime wedges, 1 large avocado peeled, seeded and diced.

Remove the skin from the turkey and discard. Place the turkey in a large Dutch oven or large lidded pot. Add the salt, black peppercorns, coriander seed, cumin seed, oregano, brown sugar, cinnamon stick, hot chilies, bay leaves, and the orange and lime juice. Add enough water to just barely cover the turkey in the pot. Cover and simmer for 2 to 2½ hours, or until the meat is falling off the bone. When tender, remove the turkey from the pot and let cool. Shred with two forks or your fingers. Discard the bones and any tendons. You can store the meat for up to one week at this point.

To finish, add the lard to a frying pan and brown the meat so it has nice crispy ends. Serve on tortillas with accompaniments.

Adapted from the recipe by Chef John Ash and James O. Fraioli from the cookbook Wild.

WINE SUGGESTION:

Wagner Vineyards Estate Winery Cabernet Franc

As Cabernet Franc throughout the Finger Lakes region garners more and more international recognition, Wagner Vineyards continues to set the standard for the red vinifera in the region. This Cabernet Franc is barrel-aged for a year in a combination of American and French oak, resulting in subtle hints of vanilla and a long finish that complement its fruit-forward taste and blueberry aroma.

DUCK

The waterfowl family Anatidae

When it comes to native waterfowl of North America, the actual numbers of the types of ducks vary slightly from about 34 to 37 depending on certain ducks being included or excluded in several groups. The groups of waterfowl also vary from two to five. Ducks are most often categorized into either Dabblers, Divers, or Sea ducks.

THE DABBLERS

The dabbling group includes mallard, black duck, green- and blue-winged teal, gadwall, cinnamon teal, widgeon, pintail, northern shoveler, and wood duck. Albeit "woodies" are commonly called a perching duck, it is often included in the dabbling duck category. Dabbling ducks can be identified by their "duck butt." These ducks tilt their front ends down into the water to sift food through their bills. Their beaks are lined with tiny plates to catch any tasty matter. They are omnivorous eaters.

In the dabbling group, the green-winged teal, wood duck, and mallard ducks are considered the best eating ducks, in that order of preference. Green-winged teal are rated as a top-shelf tasting duck. No other dabbler beats its flavor and tenderness. Wood ducks make fine eating indeed. Their meat is tender and succulent and can be prepared in many ways. Mallards are large and provide a lot of meat, which is one reason waterfowlers shoot so many of them. The flesh has a coarse texture and can have, at times, a *slight* gamey taste, but still provides a fine-tasting meal.

THE DIVERS

Divers are mostly big-water birds that include the canvasback, redhead, scaup, ring-necked, bufflehead, goldeneye, and ruddy ducks. Diving ducks, also called sea ducks, are usually the ducks that inhabit giant bodies of water like large deep lakes, wide rivers, coastal bays, and inlets. Their secondary wing feathers are typically not as bright as those on the dabbler ducks. All diving ducks do as they are named for: they dive for their food, completely submerging their bodies. The most sought-after divers as table fare, however, are canvasbacks, redheads, and the greater and lesser scaup.

THE SEA DUCKS

This group should be called a tribe, as they are a numerous bunch indeed. Sea ducks include scoters, eiders, mergansers, goldeneyes, black scoter, bufflehead, old-squaws, Labrador, smew, and harlequin ducks. All are primarily sea ducks found along both coasts of North America. Scoters are coastal ducks. Eiders are primarily Arctic and Alaskan ducks. The harlequin is as colorful as the wood duck, and the oldsquaw is found in the extreme northern regions of the east and west coasts as well as the Great Lakes.

Waterfowl and migratory game bird seasons generally occur in the fall and early winter months. Since the numbers and varieties of ducks are numerous, hunters much check both the federal and state game laws prior to hunting for bag limits, hunting hours, methods, firearms, etc. Hunting tactics for all duck species include using duck calls, decoys, blinds, the ability to quickly identify ducks as they fly by and, of course, a well-trained retrieving dog. Standard equipment includes a shotgun with appropriate choke, waterfowl loads, hip boot waders, sturdy game bags, and a sturdy boat. Waterfowl hunters are the supermen (and women) of all hunters. To bag their prey, they must, and do, endure the harshest weather conditions Mother Nature can throw at them (rain, sleet, snow, wind, fog, and even being sprayed with water by the dog). Ducks don't fly much on warm, blue bird days—eh? Therefore, how much clothing and what kind of clothing worn will have a considerable influence on a waterfowler's comfort and time in the blind.

CANVASBACK

Aythya vallisneria

There is one duck that should never be overlooked as prime-tasting waterfowl, and that's the Canvasback (a.k.a. cans). They are the largest of diving ducks in North America. They measure about 20 to 22 inches long and averagely weigh about 3.5 pounds. The canvasback's migration takes it through the Mississippi Flyway to their wintering grounds in the mid-Atlantic US, or the Pacific Flyway (which is the major north-south flyway for migratory birds in America) to the canvasbacks wintering grounds along the coast of California.

Although canvasbacks are highly prized for their *very* tasty flesh, bagging them for the table can be challenging. They have the fastest timed flight speed of any duck, making them hell-on-wings for hunters to connect with!

There is a saying among experienced waterfowl hunters that goes: *Only foolish duck hunters pass up any opportunity to shoot and eat canvasbacks!* No duck has ever achieved a higher status rating as table fare than the exquisite-tasting canvasback. In days of old, cans were considered a meal for the rich and famous and they were once referred to as "the duck of royalty." The can has scores of waterfowl hunters that all agree: it has achieved the apex level of culinary savor—no other duck can lay claim to this. An animal's diet typically determines the flavor and tenderness of their meat. However, when it comes to what canvasbacks eat, their diet doesn't really seem to matter. They simply taste different and better than other ducks. Their meat is a rich crimson; their skin is pinkish toned. It can't be said enough, from field to fork, canvasbacks are a rare culinary treat.

ROASTED WILD MALLARD
WITH A SIMPLE RED WINE SAUCE

SERVES 6

1 mallard duck ready to roast,
    feather and guts removed

Salt and black pepper

2 bay leaves

1 sprig thyme

2 cloves garlic, peeled

6 juniper berries

1 tablespoon of duck fat, or
    olive oil

1 shallot diced

1 glass red wine

1 cup chicken stock or water

1 tablespoon unsalted butter,
    optional

Braised Savoy cabbage, optional

Roasted potatoes in duck fat,
    optional

Preheat the oven at 450°F.

Season the duck with salt and black pepper. Stuff the inside of the duck with bay leaves, thyme, garlic, and juniper berries. Heat the duck fat or olive oil in a heavy skillet over medium heat, and sauté the duck until crisp on all sides, about 10 minutes. Place in the oven, and roast for 15 to 20 minutes for rare to medium rare.

Remove the duck from the oven, place on a large plate, cover, and let rest breast-side down for 5 minutes. Debone the duck completely and keep breast and leg meat covered. Chop up the carcass bones and add them to the skillet over medium heat. Brown the bones, turning often. Add the diced shallots, cook 5 more minutes, and deglaze the pan with the glass of red wine. Reduce the wine till almost dry, then add the chicken stock. Reduce the heat and let simmer until half reduced, about 30 minutes. Strain and finish the sauce with butter.

Reheat the breasts and legs, slice the breast, and pour the hot sauce over the duck. I usually serve this duck with braised Savoy cabbage and roasted potatoes in duck fat. This dish is also delicious without the sauce—just deglaze the skillet with a little water.

Adapted from the recipe by Chef John Ash and James O. Fraioli from the cookbook Wild.

WINE SUGGESTION:

Wagner Vineyards Estate Winery Grace House Pinot Noir

This is a delicately styled Pinot Noir complete with a full bouquet of berries, spice, and notes of cinnamon. Medium-bodied and flavorful, it pairs nicely with grilled vegetable and fish dishes, as well as savory pasta and poultry entrees.

ROAST DUCK WITH HONEY BALSAMIC GLAZE

SERVES 6

6-pound whole duck, cleaned, rinsed, and patted dry
Salt, as needed
5 cloves garlic, peeled and chopped
1 lemon, sliced
½ cup balsamic vinegar
1 lemon, juiced
¼ cup honey

WINE SUGGESTION:

Wagner Vineyards Estate Winery Semi-Dry Riesling

At just less than 2 percent residual sugar, this semi-dry expression is a classic example of the Finger Lakes' signature varietal. Rich and full-bodied with aromas and flavors of peaches and a hint of pineapple, this wine appeals to wine lovers of all palates and dishes of many flavors.

Preheat the oven to 350°F.

With a sharp knife, score the duck's skin on the breast in a diamond pattern, making sure to only cut the skin without reaching the meat. With the knifepoint, poke the other fatty parts of the duck to make sure the fat is released. Next, season the duck liberally, inside and out, with salt.

Transfer the duck to a roasting pan, breast-side up.

Place the garlic and lemon slices inside the cavity. Using butcher's twine, secure the duck legs and tuck the loose skin flap inside the duck cavity to keep the garlic and lemon inside.

Place the duck and roast pan into the preheated oven. Roast for 1 hour. After 1 hour, flip the duck over on its breast and roast breast-side down for 40 minutes. After 40 minutes, remove the duck and transfer to a platter. Pour all the pan drippings into a large heat-proof bowl or container. Return the duck to the roasting pan, breast-side up, and continue to cook in the oven for 40 minutes. Brush the duck, especially the scored areas, every 10 minutes with the balsamic vinegar and juice of 1 lemon, whisked together in a small bowl.

In another small bowl, combine the honey with the leftover balsamic-vinegar and lemon juice mixture. After 40 minutes, brush the honey mixture over the duck, especially the scored areas, and roast for an additional 40 minutes, brushing every 10 minutes. For the last 10 minutes, you can broil the duck to really crisp, but make sure not to burn the roasted bird in the process.

Remove the duck from the oven and let sit for 15 minutes. Discard the garlic and lemon and slice the duck.

Adapted from the recipe by food blog Julia's Album.

PAN-SEARED DUCK BREAST WITH PORT WINE SAUCE

SERVES 4

½ cup sugar

2 tablespoons water

½ cup red wine vinegar

¼ cup port or fortified wine

1 star anise pod, optional

4 boneless duck breast halves
    with skin

Kosher salt, to taste

Fresh cracked black pepper, to
    taste

1½ cups halved red seedless
    grapes

1 teaspoon chopped fresh
    thyme (3 sprigs)

1 cup loosely packed watercress
    leaves, optional

In a small saucepan over medium-high heat, add the sugar and water, and cook, stirring frequently, until the sugar dissolves and the mixture turns a pale golden color, 8 to 10 minutes. Remove the pan from the heat and add the vinegar. Return the pan to the heat and cook until the mixture is melted and smooth, 2 to 3 minutes. Add the wine and star anise, if using. Reduce heat to low and simmer until the liquid reduces to thin syrup, about 10 minutes. Discard the star anise. Keep the sauce warm over very low heat until ready to use.

Next, blot the duck breasts dry. Use a sharp knife to score the fat of each breast in a diamond pattern, taking care not to cut into the meat. Season both sides of each breast generously with salt and pepper, then place them skin-side down in a large, cold skillet. Place the skillet over low heat and cook for 3 minutes. Increase the heat to medium and continue cooking until the duck begins to sizzle. Continue cooking until the skin is browned, crisp, and has rendered most of its fat, 6 to 8 minutes.

Preheat the oven to 350°F.

Spoon off and reserve the fat from the skillet. Flip over the breasts and transfer the skillet to the oven and roast for 2 to 4 minutes, or until an instant-read thermometer inserted into the thickest part of the breast registers 125°F to 135°F. Transfer breasts to a plate to rest.

Add the grapes to the skillet and toss with the thyme and a pinch of salt and pepper. Roast in the oven until the grapes are hot and wrinkled in spots, 8 to 10 minutes.

Transfer breasts to plate and spoon the grapes and sauce over the top. Garnish with a small handful of watercress, if using, and serve immediately.

Adapted from the recipe by food blogger Alexandra Stafford and Alexandra's Kitchen.

WINE SUGGESTION:

Wagner Vineyards Estate Winery Meritage

This Cabernet Sauvignon–dominant blend includes Bordeaux standbys Cabernet Franc and Merlot and is only produced as a result of ideal growing seasons that yield exceptional vinifera. Only four of the past fifteen years have made the cut: 2007, 2010, 2012, and 2016. This superb Finger Lakes red may be enjoyed now or aged and is a perfect dinner wine to serve with hearty dishes.

GOOSE

Anatidae

There are several types of goose in North America, but waterfowl hunters concentrate most on four species: the Canada goose, white-fronted goose, snow goose, and brant. Most waterfowlers focus their attention on hunting the Canada goose, as they are the most widely distributed, populated, and common of all the goose species.

WHITE-FRONTED GOOSE

Anser albifrons

White-Fronted geese are more commonly known as specklebelly. Waterfowlers consider speckle-bellies a very popular goose to hunt. They wing into the continental United States generally in November from their breeding grounds in Arctic Canada and Alaska. Flocks of the mid-continent population are found in Oklahoma, Mississippi, Alabama, and several Atlantic coastal states. The largest wintering flocks are found in southeast Texas, Louisiana, and eastern Arkansas. The Pacific population of white-fronted geese winter in the Central Valley of California. Specklebellies are sometimes hunted incidentally when waterfowlers find them mixed in with large flocks of snow geese. The specklebelly is a large bird, about 27 to 29 inches tall and weighs about 4 to 6 pounds. As table fare, specklebellies are said to be delicious—and they are indeed.

SNOW GOOSE

Anser caerulescen

Snow geese (a.k.a. Snows) breed north of the timberline in Alaska, Canada, and Greenland. Snows winter in warm parts of North America. There are two species: the lesser and greater. The lesser is about 30 inches tall and weighs 4 to 6 pounds. The greater stands about 2.5 feet tall and is a heftier bird, weighing about 7 pounds on average. The lesser migrates along the Central, Mississippi, and Pacific Flyways. The greater migrates the Atlantic Flyway.

Snows travel in huge flocks; that's a lot of eyeballs investigating for potential danger. They have excellent memories and, once shot at, they will rarely return to the same place. A set of decoys generally results in two, tops three, successful hunts; an evening, morning, and *possibly* another evening. After that, kiss the snow geese adieu and start looking for another hotspot to hunt them.

The rumor is snow geese aren't good to eat. But most waterfowlers claim they can be quite flavorsome when prepared properly. Always skin the snows; it will prevent any off-putting flavor that resides in the skin.

BRANT

Branta bernicla

Brant are more correctly referred to as sea brant. Basically, they are an ocean-going goose. They are small for geese at only 22 to 26 inches tall and weighing only about 3½ pounds. As far as taste, Brant tend to absorb the flavor of whatever they eat. Brant eat grasses, green algae, pondweed, some fish, and a lot of eelgrass, where herring have deposited their eggs. Brant are challenging not only to hunt but can also test a cook's skills to yield tasty table fare. Need I say more?

CANADA GOOSE

Branta canadensis

Canada geese are native to North America and inhabit the entire continent. It is the largest subspecies of goose. Canada goose (a.k.a. Honker) is one of the most recognized waterfowl birds in North America. In fall, this migratory waterfowl can be heard honking as they fly overhead in their familiar V-shaped formation. The call of the Canada goose is a staple of fall. Its rhythmic honking leaves goosebumps on both hunters and nonhunters alike. There is no question that Canada goose is the undeniable king of its domain. With more than 5 million breeding Canada Geese in North America, they are the most hunted and eaten species of geese.

Over the last decade, hunting for Canada geese has become a highly generalized sport and hugely popular. It requires a combination of good tactics, equipment, and a dogged determination to outsmart these wary birds. Hunting honkers successfully means knowing the varied tactics and having the right equipment. It is critical to learn the different goose calls and how to best use them. Hunters, firearms, and blinds must be thoroughly camouflaged. Having a lot of decoys is an absolute must.

Canada goose flesh is a lean, dark, rich meat that some waterfowl hunters go as far as saying it's "akin to roast beef." That may be a stretch. Others claim it tastes like a dark, tender cut of smoked (yup) chicken. When prepared correctly, the meat of a Canada goose can be a gastronomically pleasing meal.

WILD GOOSE HAM OR PASTRAMI

MAKES 2 CURED BREASTS

Brine:

2 quarts water

¾ cup kosher salt

¾ cup brown sugar

3 teaspoons pink salt* (sodium nitrite)

½ cup Port or Madeira

1 bunch fresh thyme

2 large bay leaves

1 tablespoon juniper berries

2 teaspoons black peppercorns

1 tablespoon chopped sage

2 large Canada (or other) goose breasts

*Note: Pink salt (not Himalayan pink salt) is used in most smoking recipes. This salt is an insurance against botulism, especially when smoking below 300°F.

In a large pot, add the water, salt, sugar, pink salt, port or Madeira, thyme, bay leaves, juniper berries, black peppercorns, and sage. Bring to a simmer, stirring occasionally to dissolve the salt and sugar. Remove from heat, and allow to cool to room temperature, then refrigerate until completely chilled.

Add the goose breasts to the brine, and weigh them down with a small plate to keep them submerged. Refrigerate for 8 hours.

Rinse the breasts under cold water and pat dry. Refrigerate on a rack set over a rimmed plate or baking sheet for at least 8 hours, up to 24.

Hot smoke the breasts to an internal temperature of 160°F, about 2½ hours. Refrigerate until ready to use.

Adapted from the recipe by Chef John Ash and James O. Fraioli from the cookbook Wild.

WINE SUGGESTION:

Wagner Vineyards Estate Winery Caywood East Dry Riesling

For more than ninety years, the steep slopes of Wagner's Caywood East vineyard have produced exceptional grapes. Replanted entirely to Riesling in 2005, this tradition continues. Nectarine and lime aromas, citrus, mineral flavors, and a crisp, clean finish make this dry Riesling a superb enhancement for seafood, poultry, and other light meals.

GOOSE RAGÙ WITH POLENTA

SERVES 6

⅓ cup olive oil

12 ounces boneless, skinless goose breast, very finely chopped

6 ounces goose liver, very finely chopped

1 cup finely diced onion

½ cup finely chopped celery

½ cup finely chopped carrot

1 tablespoon finely chopped garlic

1½ tablespoons finely chopped fresh rosemary

1 teaspoon fennel seeds

½ teaspoon crushed red chili flakes, or to taste

1 cup dry white wine

1 can (28-ounce) whole peeled tomatoes, preferably San Marzano

Soft Polenta

1 cup whole milk

4 cups water

1 cup Polenta cornmeal

Salt and freshly ground pepper

Butter

Freshly grated Parmesan or Pecorino

Heat 2 tablespoons of olive oil in a heavy deep saucepan over medium-high heat. Add the breast meat and cook until browned, about 5 minutes. Transfer to a bowl, add the liver, and cook until it is just browned, about 4 minutes. Add the liver to the bowl with the cooked breast meat. Add the remaining oil to the pan, and cook the onions, celery, carrot, and garlic until lightly browned, about 7 minutes.

Stir in the rosemary, fennel, and chili flakes, and cook a couple more minutes. Add the wine, and cook until the liquid is nearly evaporated, about 5 minutes. Meanwhile, crush the tomatoes with your hands, and add the tomatoes, stock, reserved goose breast and liver, salt and pepper to taste, and cook until thickened, about 20 minutes over moderate heat.

Taste one more time for seasoning.

To make the polenta, bring the milk and water to a boil in a medium-sized heavy-bottomed saucepan over high heat. Add 1 teaspoon salt. Slowly pour the cornmeal into the water, stirring with a wire whisk or wooden spoon. Continue stirring as mixture thickens, 2 to 3 minutes.

Turn the heat to low so the mixture barely simmers. Cook for at least 20 minutes, stirring every few minutes to make sure the polenta isn't sticking to the bottom of the pan. If the polenta becomes very thick, thin with ½ cup water, stir well, and continue cooking. Add up to another cup of water, if necessary, to keep the polenta soft enough to stir.

Carefully taste, making sure the grains are tender. Season to your taste with salt and pepper. Stir in a couple of tablespoons of butter, and serve immediately, or cover and set saucepan in a pot of barely simmering water for up to 2 hours. Add additional water or milk, if necessary, to keep the soft consistency. Stir in cheese to your taste just before serving.

Spoon the polenta into wide bowls, spoon the Ragù on top, and garnish with a healthy sprinkling of Pecorino.

Adapted from the recipe by Chef John Ash and James O. Fraioli from the cookbook Wild.

WINE SUGGESTION:

Wagner Vineyards Estate Winery Reserve Chardonnay

Chardonnay is the second most commonly planted white vinifera varietal grown in the Finger Lakes, as it grows well in cool climates. Wagner's Reserve Chardonnay blends both unoaked and barrel-aged juice to produce layers of complexity and a smooth finish that pairs perfectly with flavorful poultry dishes.

SLOW COOKER GOOSE BREASTS

SERVES 4

1–2 tablespoons cooking oil

4 Canada goose breasts,
 cleaned and trimmed

1 package Lipton's Dry Onion
 Soup Mix

1 cup water

1 (15-ounce) can crushed
 tomatoes

1 cup diced potatoes

1 cup sliced carrots

1 cup sliced celery

1 tablespoon dried oregano

Salt and fresh cracked black
 pepper to taste

Wild rice cooked to package
 instructions, for serving

Add the oil to a large skillet over medium-high heat. When oil is hot, add the goose breasts and sear until brown on both sides.

Remove the browned breasts from the skillet and transfer to a slow cooker or crockpot. Add the Lipton's Dry Onion Soup Mix and water and stir well. Cook on low for 4 hours.

After 4 hours, add the crushed tomatoes, potatoes, carrots, celery, oregano, salt, and pepper. Stir well and continue to cook for 4 to 6 hours, or until the goose is extremely tender.

Serve with wild rice.

Adapted from the recipe by Lord Cheseline and Gourmay.net.

WINE SUGGESTION:

Wagner Vineyards Estate Winery Merlot

An exceptional representation of a cool-climate Merlot, this medium-bodied wine features aromas of cherry and dark stone fruit with classic flavors of black cherry and plum. This versatile wine will go well with most meals—try it with grilled red meats, poultry, and savory vegetarian dishes.

REPTILES & AMPHIBIANS

AMERICAN ALLIGATOR

Alligator mississippiensis

Alligators are top reptilian predators that first appeared on the planet about 100 million years ago during the late Cretaceous period. Nowadays, the American alligator is commonly referred to as alligator and/or gator. They are the largest living reptile relative of the dinosaurs that went extinct 65 million years ago. The American alligator shouldn't be confused with the American crocodile. American gators are a large species of crocodilian and are the second-largest species in Alligatoridae family. Adult male alligators can reach lengths of 15 feet and more and can weigh more than 1,000 pounds. Females are smaller, rarely measuring more than 10 feet long. An adult American alligator's bite force can be about 2,125 pounds per square inch; it's the third most powerful animal bite in the world.

American alligators are indigenous to several states including Florida, Virginia, North Carolina, Texas, Alabama, Mississippi, Arkansas, Oklahoma, and northwestern Tennessee. They inhabit bogs, wetlands, swamps, ponds, lakes, clearwater streams, and rivers. While alligators prefer fresh water, they are sometimes found in brackish water (brackish water is saltier than freshwater but not as salty as ocean water).

In the past, unregulated hunting negatively affected American alligator populations throughout their range. By 1967, it was listed as an endangered species, and in 1973 it was listed as a protected species. Amazingly, just 14 years later (1987), the United States Fish and Wildlife Service (USFWS) removed the American alligator from the endangered species list, as it was deemed to be "fully" recovered. To make that point, today there are 1.3 million alligators in the state of Florida alone!

As seen on many reality television shows, alligator hunting is legal with the appropriate licenses and tags. Outdoorsmen can buy alligator hunting licenses in Florida, Georgia, Alabama, Arkansas, Mississippi, Louisiana, North Carolina, South Carolina, and Texas. There are many ways to hunt alligators. But they are very dangerous animals and should not be hunted without an experienced licensed guide—at least until the hunter develops a considerable amount of hunting experience. There are countless outfitters that can be researched on the web. Alligators are hunted to keep the population numbers healthy and in check. Their hides are valuable and should be cared for accordingly soon after the hunt.

Alligator meat is an important part of Southern cuisine, and therein lies a primary reason it is hunted throughout the south so diligently. Alligator is a healthy meat due to its high protein and low-fat content. It is said that a 3.5-ounce serving has about 145 calories, 28 grams of protein,

3 percent fat, and 67 milligrams of cholesterol. It also contains a significant amount of minerals like niacin, potassium, phosphorus, vitamin B12, and monounsaturated fatty acids.

Alligator meat's taste and flavor is often described as—yup, you guessed it—"chicken," but mixed with a faint taste of fish. (Huh?) It has also been said to taste like quail. Well, at least not everyone says it tastes like chicken! On a more serious note, alligator meat can be chewy, and it does have an ever-so-slight hint of a fishy flavor. But that depends on what type of water the alligator was taken in. Stagnant waters can cause alligator meat to have slightly fishy taste, just as it makes frogs, crayfish, turtle, and certain fish taste like the water they came from. The cooler and faster the water, the better the taste of the alligator meat.

Alligator must be quickly field dressed and cooled properly, preferably put on ice as soon as possible to preserve the meat's tenderness and flavor. If they lie dead in a boat for hours, it won't enhance the tenderness and flavor of the meat. There are many different methods of preparation and cooking alligator meat, including marinating, tenderizing, deep frying, stewing, roasting, smoking, and sautéing. Alligator meat is a longtime historical staple when making gumbo and traditional Creole dishes of Louisiana, and both are quite delicious. Going the extra yard to take care of the meat from the moment the gator is killed to seasoning and cooking the meat properly in the kitchen will provide a wonderful dish that whets the palate of even the most finicky taste buds—fishy or otherwise.

Alligator Gumbo

ALLIGATOR GUMBO

SERVES 15

4 tablespoons salted butter

1 cup chopped bell pepper

1 cup chopped white onion

2 cups chopped celery

½ cup all-purpose flour

2 (28-ounce) cans crushed
   tomatoes

3 dashes Tony Chachere's
   Original Creole Seasoning

2 tablespoons brown sugar

3 bay leaves

8 cloves

⅓ teaspoon hot pepper sauce

4 pounds alligator meat,
   chopped into bite-sized
   pieces

1 tablespoon lemon juice

⅔ cup white wine

Cooked steamed rice, as
   needed, optional

In a Dutch oven over medium heat, melt the butter and then add the bell pepper, onions, and celery. Sauté for 10 minutes, or until the vegetables are tender. Add the flour and blend thoroughly. Add the tomatoes gradually while stirring. Add the creole seasoning, sugar, bay leaves, cloves, and hot pepper sauce. Bring to a boil. Add the alligator meat to the mixture and return to a boil. Reduce the heat to low and simmer, uncovered, for 45 minutes, stirring occasionally. Remove from the heat and discard the bay leaves and cloves. Stir in the lemon juice and white wine.

Serve over steamed rice, if desired.

Adapted from the recipe by Tony Chachere's Famous Creole Cuisine.

WINE SUGGESTION:

2017 J. Lohr Estates Seven Oaks Cabernet Sauvignon

The 2017 J. Lohr Estates Seven Oaks Cabernet Sauvignon is dark and dense in color to the rim of the glass. Layered aromas of black cherry, currant, and blueberry are accented by an authentic barrel-aged bouquet of dark chocolate, cocoa powder, and roasted coffee. The palate peaks with high-toned red berry fruit and follows with bright acidity and a full structure that is both dense and soft at once.

BLACKENED ALLIGATOR WITH COCONUT RUM SAUCE AND MANGO RELISH

SERVES 4

2 large mangoes, peeled and
thinly sliced

½ cup sweet peppers, seeded
and thinly sliced

2 tablespoons finely chopped
fresh cilantro

1 lime, juiced

Salt and black pepper, to taste

1 cup dark rum

1 teaspoon pure vanilla extract

1 cup coconut milk

1 cup heavy cream

1 tablespoon cooking oil

1 pound alligator tail meat,
thinly sliced

1 tablespoon blackened spice
mix

To make the relish, in a medium bowl, add the mango, sweet pepper, cilantro, and lime juice and season with salt and pepper. Set aside.

Preheat a medium sauté pan over medium heat. Remove the pan and carefully add the rum (being extremely careful) to the hot pan, then return to the heat. Cook down until the rum has reduced by half. Add the vanilla, coconut milk, and heavy cream and stir to combine. Reduce the heat to low and cook until the Coconut Rum Sauce is thick and coats the back of a spoon. Transfer to a bowl and set aside.

Wipe out the pan and reheat over medium-high heat. Add the oil. While the oil is heating, lightly season both sides of the sliced alligator tail with the blackened spice mix. Pan sear both sides of the alligator for 30 seconds to 1 minute; do not overcrowd the pan. Remove the alligator from the pan and repeat the process until all the alligator is cooked.

Serve warm with Coconut Rum Sauce and Mango Relish.

Adapted from the recipe by Fresh from Florida & Florida Department of Agriculture & Consumer Services.

WINE SUGGESTION:

2017 J. Lohr Arroyo Vista Chardonnay

Light straw in color, this Chardonnay exhibits intriguing aromas of Meyer lemon cream, yellow flowers, baked pear, crème brûlée, and toasted hazelnuts. The rich palate texture is derived from the use of classic Burgundian techniques, such as primary and malolactic fermentation in French oak barrels and weekly stirring of the lees during aging. The texture is balanced by fresh flavors of apple, pear, and citrus, with a long, sweet oak finish.

FRIED ALLIGATOR WITH HONEY MUSTARD SAUCE

SERVES 6

6 tablespoons honey

3 tablespoons Dijon mustard

2 tablespoons mayonnaise

1 tablespoon fresh chopped
Italian flat-leaf parsley

Cayenne pepper, to taste

Salt and black pepper, divided,
to taste

Cooking oil, as needed, for
frying

4 cups cornmeal

2 cups buttermilk

1 pound alligator nuggets,
defrosted or fresh, pounded
slightly to tenderize

To make the sauce, in a small bowl, add the honey, mustard, mayonnaise, parsley, cayenne, salt, and pepper. Mix well to combine. Adjust seasoning if necessary and set aside.

Preheat a deep fryer (or suitable pot filled halfway with vegetable or peanut oil, and using a candy thermometer) to 350°F.

Place the cornmeal and buttermilk in separate bowls and season with salt and pepper. Dip each alligator nugget into the cornmeal and then into the buttermilk. Let the buttermilk drain slightly, then dip the nugget back into cornmeal. Shake off excess cornmeal. Repeat the process until all the alligator nuggets are coated. Fry for 2 to 3 minutes or until the nuggets are golden-brown and completely cooked. Fry in batches if necessary, and do not overcook alligator meat, as it can become chewy. Transfer the nuggets to a plate lined with paper towels to drain. Serve warm with the Honey Mustard Sauce.

Adapted from the recipe by Fresh from Florida & Florida Department of Agriculture & Consumer Services.

WINE SUGGESTION:

2019 J. Lohr Estates Flume Crossing Sauvignon Blanc

The 2019 Flume Crossing Sauvignon Blanc is pale yellow in color, highlighted by aromas of honeysuckle and daffodil, grapefruit, sweet herbs, and key lime. These aromas are complemented on the palate by the bright flavors of grapefruit, lime, and lemongrass, with the rich texture and long finish provided by the acacia barrels.

AMERICAN BULLFROG

Lithobates catesbeianus

The American bullfrog (a.k.a. bullfrog) is a member of the family Ranidae, or "true frogs." In the United States, bullfrogs inhabit all fifty states. In Canada, bullfrogs are found mostly in the eastern provinces. Wherever they are found, the bullfrog is considered an invasive species.

Bullfrogs inhabit large lakes, ponds, and other permanent bodies of water. They are also found in streams, creeks, and swamps close to the water's edge, typically pointing their heads facing out into the water. Male bullfrogs make a deep guttural baritone vocalization that mimics the sound of a bull cow. They will croak throughout the day and night; however, they are much more vocal at night. Their reverberating call can be heard for up to a half-mile away. They are the largest of all North American frogs and can reach a length of 8 inches or more and weigh up to 1.5 pounds. That's a lot of frog.

The giant bullfrog is a stone-cold killer. It will ambush almost any animal it can fit into its mouth and swallow. Bullfrogs commonly eat insects, crayfish, salamanders, fish, lizards, worms, snakes, small turtles, small mammals, birds, and even other frogs. High on the bullfrog's menu are newly hatched ducklings and, sometimes, tiny goslings, as well, putting bullfrogs on the "most wanted" list of waterfowl enthusiasts under the guise of—eat the enemy!

Nevertheless, the bullfrog has an equally large number of predatory enemies as well. A wide variety of fish, lizards, birds, muskrats, skunk, fox, racoons, and various other animals eat bullfrogs, their eggs, and tadpoles. Bullfrogs are a favorite snack of the deadly predator water bird, a.k.a. the blue heron.

Another more cunning predator of bullfrogs includes the highly intelligent species known as *Homo sapiens*. That's because humans have figured out bullfrog legs are prized meat. So, the clever *Homo sapiens*, being hunters and gatherers as they are, have added frog legs to their menu.

Before going out to stalk bullfrogs, always check all state game laws related to hunting frogs. Successful hunting of bullfrogs takes only locating good bullfrog habitat. That should take all of sixty seconds. Seriously, they are not hard to find. Most times their incessant croaking will give them away. Look for them in places where there are cattails and similar pond vegetation. Bullfrogs prefer living in waters without a current, but they can also be found in waterways with *light* currents. While bullfrogs can be caught during daylight, hunters will increase their catch ten-fold by hunting them at night.

Hunters should move along the shoreline slowly and quietly. At night, bullfrogs are more easily spotted by using an LED flashlight and shining the beam along the banks of ponds and other waterways. Shine the light directly into the bullfrog's eyes; this tactic is called *Jacking*. The light will make the bullfrog go into a trance. It can now be caught by hand or by using a tool known as a frog gig—a long, stout stick fitted with a five-point pitchfork (the two-point gig doesn't work well to spear and hold large bullfrogs). Other equipment includes a pair of hip waders, extra flashlight batteries, and a lightweight, *clean* plastic bucket, with a lid.

It is widely known that bullfrog legs are considered a delicacy of French and Chinese cuisines. They are also served at many fashionable restaurants within the United States as part of a high-end exquisite meal. A lot of people who eat bullfrogs compare the taste to the white meat of (oh no—not again)—chicken! I suppose that's said because frog legs can have a mild texture and flavor that is said to taste like chicken wings.

Truth be told, bullfrog meat doesn't look or taste like chicken wings, chicken breasts, or any other part of a chicken. The taste and texture are more akin to the white flesh of some ducks and a mild flavor of fish. The key factor in the flavor, consistency, and tenderness of *wild* bullfrog legs is most definitely related to the type of water they are caught in. Stagnant, muddy water will result in frog meat tasting funky and having a more pungent odor. Better tasting frog meat will be from bullfrogs caught in clean waters, and finer tasting wild frog meat is from bullfrogs caught in clear water with a slight current. The best of the best frog meat, however, comes from farm-raised bull-frogs. Whether fried, sautéed, slow-cooked in a gumbo, or smoked, frog legs are a scrumptious dish.

Fried Frog Legs

FRIED FROG LEGS

SERVES 12 AS AN APPETIZER

24 prepared frogs legs (pairs if small)

Fresh milk

3 cups dry white wine

4 sprigs flat-leaf parsley plus 2 tablespoons chopped, for garnish

1 small onion, peeled and sliced

Grated nutmeg, as needed

Sea salt and freshly cracked pepper (preferably white)

1 cup flour

Peanut oil, as needed, for frying

Lemon wedges, as needed, for garnish

Soak the frog legs in milk, covered, for at least 1 hour. This will help draw out any impurities and whiten and swell the legs. Drain the legs, wash well, and pat dry.

Add the wine, parsley sprigs, onion, a big pinch of grated nutmeg, and a bit of salt and pepper to a large bowl. Add the frog legs and let them marinate for 1 hour, turning 2 or 3 times. Drain and dry the legs, then dust them with flour, shaking off any excess.

Add 1 inch of oil to a deep saucepan, and heat to 350°F. Fry the legs until nicely browned, in batches, if necessary. Sprinkle with chopped parsley, salt, and pepper, and serve with lemon wedges to squeeze over.

Adapted from the recipe by Chef John Ash and James O. Fraioli from the cookbook Wild.

WINE SUGGESTION:

2018 J. Lohr Estates Riverstone Chardonnay

The 2018 Riverstone Chardonnay exhibits youthful hues of light straw. The enticing aromas are reminiscent of white peach, apricot, ripe orange, and cocoa, and complemented by the palate flavors of citrus cream and nectarine. The rich texture and balance on the palate from aging *sur lie* gives way to flavors of vanilla, crème brûlée, and a hint of oak on the long finish.

TERIYAKI FROG LEGS WITH MUSHROOMS

SERVES 4

¼ cup unsalted butter

2 cups chopped yellow onions

1 cup chopped red or green bell pepper

1 cup freshly minced Italian flat-leaf parsley

1 pound sliced cremini mushrooms

2 tablespoons minced garlic

1½ teaspoons onion powder

½ teaspoon ground ginger

1 teaspoon hot sauce

2 cups boned frog legs

½ cup dry white wine

½ cup teriyaki sauce

Green onions, minced, as needed

Buttered grits, optional, for serving

Stewed tomatoes, optional, for serving

In a large wok or skillet, melt the butter over medium-high heat. Add the onions, bell peppers, and parsley, sautéing until the onions are translucent. Add the mushrooms, garlic, onion powder, and ground ginger. Stir well and cook until the mushrooms are warmed through. Add the hot sauce and frog legs and stir well, then add the wine and teriyaki sauce. Reduce the heat to medium-low and simmer for 10 minutes, stirring once or twice. Garnish with minced green onions and serve with buttered grits and stewed tomatoes, if desired.

Adapted from the recipe by Rick Browne.

WINE SUGGESTION:

2018 J. Lohr Estates Bay Mist White Riesling

The 2018 J. Lohr Estates Bay Mist White Riesling is pale straw in color, offering aromas of paperwhites, daffodil, ripe apple, Meyer lemon, and lychee. These delicious aromas are complemented on the palate by cool climate minerality, rich texture, and a spritz of natural carbonation on the finish.

CAJUN-FRIED BULLFROG LEGS

SERVES 4

2 egg whites

1 tablespoon Cajun seasoning

1 teaspoon cayenne pepper

1 teaspoon lemon pepper

1 teaspoon salt

2 tablespoons Tabasco sauce

1 teaspoon baking powder

4 ounces fresh beer

2 tablespoons cornstarch

2 cups all-purpose flour

1 cup yellow corn meal

12 pairs bullfrog legs, cleaned and skinned

1 quart peanut oil

In a bowl, add the egg whites, Cajun seasoning, cayenne pepper, lemon pepper, salt, Tabasco sauce, baking powder, and beer. Mix until well combined. Next, dissolve the cornstarch in a small amount of cold water and add to the mixture. Blend all of the ingredients together.

In a separate bowl, mix together the flour and corn meal.

Dredge the frog legs in the beer batter, then in the flour-cornmeal mixture, coating all sides.

Preheat a deep fryer (or suitable pot filled halfway with the peanut oil, and using a candy thermometer) to 365°F.

Fry the legs for 3 to 4 minutes or until the legs are golden-brown and completely cooked. Fry in batches, if necessary, as not to overcrowd and lower the oil temperature. Transfer the legs to a plate lined with paper towels to drain. Serve warm with your favorite dipping sauce.

Adapted from the recipe by Jacques Gaspard.

WINE SUGGESTION:

2018 J. Lohr Estates Falcon's Perch Pinot Noir

The 2018 J. Lohr Estates Falcon's Perch showcases the best of cool climate Monterey County Pinot Noir. Wild strawberry and sage on the nose are followed by bright rhubarb, camphor, and dried cherry on the finish.

AMERICAN RATTLESNAKE

Crotalus cersates

Holy slithering, Batman! There are twelve different rattlesnakes in the continental United States. These include the Eastern Rattlesnake, Cranebrake, Eastern Diamondback, Western Diamondback, Mojave Rattlesnake, Tiger Rattlesnake, Eastern Massasauga, Sidewinder, Banded Rock Rattlesnake, and the Hog- and Twin-Spotted Rattlesnakes. There are also Western Rattlesnakes (five subspecies), Pygmy Rattlesnakes (three subspecies), and Nosed Rattlesnakes (two subspecies). But, for the sake of simplicity, the listed rattlers and their subspecies are all basically hunted and prepared similarly.

As the name implies, rattlesnakes were given their name from the set of rattles they accumulate at the end of their tail (segments of keratin, the same material that fingernails are made of). Each year, rattlesnakes develop a new additional rattle. When threatened, the snake aggressively shakes its tail, causing the rattles to loudly vibrate.

Rattlesnakes are the number one reptile responsible for venomous snakebites to humans throughout North America. Luckily, they rarely strike without provocation. Their toxin is potent. If the bite is treated with an antivenom serum as soon as possible, however, it is seldom fatal. Rattler venom is hemotoxic, destroying tissue that causes cell damage and blood clotting to its victim. Rattlers, like the Tiger and some Mojave Rattlesnakes, have a presynaptic neurotoxic venom (known as Mojave type-A toxin). It affects the nervous system, causing severe paralysis. Tiger rattlers have the most potent venom of all rattlesnakes in the United States.

Hunting rattlesnakes is dangerous. Records indicate that at least seven thousand people are bitten by rattlesnakes in the United States every year, accounting for several fatalities. When hunting rattlers, take every serious precaution to avoid getting bit. Survival from a rattlesnake bite that delivers venom depends on getting antivenom treatment as quickly as possible. Antivenom provided within a couple hours of a bite has a recovery probability of more than 99 percent.

To hunt rattlesnakes safely and successfully, a hunter must first undertake many safety measures. High on the list is making sure local hospitals within the hunting area have rattlesnake antivenom serum in stock. It is also necessary to have several high-quality tools including snake boots, chaps, gloves, safety snake-pouches, a 6-foot snake tong, a snake hook, and a sharp knife and/or axe.

Never hunt rattlers alone. The best locations to find rattlesnakes include dry places where their favorite prey (mice and rats) tend to hide like abandoned barns and outbuildings, rock quarries, undisturbed brush piles, rat nests, under ledges and large flat rocks. Never poke around with your hands in potential areas, especially when moving rocks, without using a large stout stick to move the rocks first. Rattlers come out of their dens or pits when there is warm weather. When in rattler country, watch your every step. Look around before moving, as one of their main defenses—camouflage—works to their advantage when they are the prey.

There are many different laws concerning the hunting of pit vipers. Each state has its own set of regulations, seasons, licenses, permits, etc. Other states don't allow hunting for rattlers at all. Therefore, it is imperative to check the governing laws before hunting for rattlesnakes in any state.

Rattlesnake meat is white. Rattler meat has a lot of tiny bones. In some recipes, all bones must be removed; yet, other recipes recommend preparing rattler meat without removing the bones. Adult rattlers have a long boneless backstrap that runs along the entire backbone. Once the rattler is cooked, the backstrap meat comes out easily. Many recipes call for southern fried snake meat. Rattler meat can also be slow cooked in a crockpot, boiled, baked, or simmered in a large pot for a couple hours. Like alligator, rattlesnake makes excellent deboned meat when used in chili.

Rattlesnake meat is highly prized as a delicacy in the southwest. It can be favorably compared to eating frog legs, alligator meat, and, some say, turtle. What it doesn't taste like, though, is chicken! While it does have a gamey flavor, cooked properly and spiced accordingly, rattler meat can provide a hunter quite a culinary treat.

DRIED BLUEBERRY AND PEPPERCORN-RUBBED RATTLESNAKE

SERVES 6

1 rattlesnake, about 4 feet, cleaned, gutted, and skinned, with head and rattler removed
¼ cup dried (or dehydrated) blueberries
1 tablespoon kosher salt
1 tablespoon cracked pepper
Zest of 1 orange

Soak the cleaned snake meat in water in the refrigerator for several hours or overnight. Remove from water and pat dry.

Heat an outdoor grill or barbecue to medium-high heat. Prepare the grill by brushing with oil or using grill nonstick spray.

While the grill is heating, add the dried blueberries to a mortar and pestle or spice grinder and grind the berries into a fine powder.

In a small bowl, add the blueberry powder along with the salt, pepper, and orange zest. Mix well to combine.

Rub the snake liberally with the Dried Blueberry and Peppercorn Rub. Coil the snake like a coil of sausage and skewer the meat in a couple places with kabob skewers so the coil stays intact. Place the coil on the hot grill, rib side down. Close the lid of the grill or barbecue and let cook for 5 minutes. Turn the snake over and cook for another 5 minutes, or until the meat is tender and begins to pull away from the bones.

Remove from the grill and let rest for 5 minutes before serving. The meat should easily peel off the backbone and ribs in large patches.

Note: When eating rattlesnake, it's best to use your fingers to pull and tear the meat away from the bones.

Adapted from the recipe by Randy King, Chef in the Wild.

WINE SUGGESTION:

J. Lohr Estates South Ridge Syrah

Varietal aromas of blueberry, lilac, and black tea meld with notes of cocoa powder and tar from one year of barrel aging in a blend of American and French oak barrels. The spice and structure of the Syrah and Mourvèdre red varieties in this blend are lifted by a touch of floral Viognier.

RATTLESNAKE FRIED RICE

SERVES 6

1 rattlesnake, about 4 feet, cleaned, gutted, and skinned, with head and rattler removed

½ cup dried white rice

1 cup water

2 tablespoons cooking oil (or bear fat)

3 tablespoons fine diced ham

1 tablespoon fresh ginger, grated

1 clove garlic, peeled and minced

1 egg

½ cup sliced green cabbage

¼ cup shredded carrot

1 tablespoon sriracha

1½ tablespoons soy sauce

¼ cup packed fresh cilantro and mint leaves (half of each)

2 tablespoons sliced green onions

Soak the cleaned snake meat in water in the refrigerator for several hours or overnight. Remove from water and pat dry. Cut the snake meat into 1-inch pieces.

Add rice and water to a small saucepan. Heat until boiling then turn to a simmer and cover. Let the rice simmer for 10 to 15 minutes, or until the rice is cooked. Remove from heat and let stand. Do not stir.

Heat a medium-sized sauté pan or wok over medium heat. Add the oil and brown the snake sections. Remove the snake from the pan. Add the diced ham to the pan and brown. Next, add the ginger and garlic, and brown lightly. Slide all the goodies in the pan to one side and crack the egg into the pan and pop the yolk. Let the egg cook until almost set, then scramble with the ingredients in the pan. Next, add the cabbage, carrots, and cooked rice. Toss all the ingredients together. Let the rice start to brown a little while cooking, about 3 to 5 minutes. Don't stir often.

Add the sriracha and then gently pour in the soy sauce, covering as much rice as possible. Add the snake back to the pan, and then add the cilantro, mint, and green onions. Toss all together and serve hot.

Note: When eating rattlesnake, it's best to use your fingers to pull and tear the meat away from the bones.

Adapted from the recipe by Randy King, Chef in the Wild

WINE SUGGESTION:

J. Lohr Estates Bay Mist White Riesling

The 2018 J. Lohr Estates Bay Mist White Riesling is pale straw in color, offering aromas of paperwhites, daffodil, ripe apple, Meyer lemon, and lychee. These delicious aromas are complemented on the palate by cool climate minerality, rich texture, and a spritz of natural carbonation on the finish.

SOUTHERN FRIED RATTLESNAKE

SERVES 6

1 rattlesnake, about 4 feet, cleaned, gutted, and skinned, with head and rattler removed

1 egg

½ cup milk

All-purpose flour

Garlic powder, as needed, to taste

Onion powder, as needed, to taste

Salt and black pepper, as needed, to taste

Cooking oil, as needed, for frying

Soak the cleaned snake meat in water in the refrigerator for several hours or overnight. Remove from water and pat dry. Cut into 4-inch pieces.

Preheat a deep fryer (or suitable pot filled halfway with vegetable or peanut oil, and using a candy thermometer) to 350°F.

In a bowl, add the egg and milk. Whisk until well combined.

In a separate bowl, add the flour, garlic powder, onion powder, salt, and pepper. Mix well until combined.

Dip each piece of rattlesnake into the egg wash and then into the seasoned flour. Shake off excess flour. Repeat the process until all the pieces are coated. Fry for 2 to 3 minutes or until the pieces are golden-brown and completely cooked. Fry in batches, if necessary. Transfer the nuggets to a plate lined with paper towels to drain. Serve warm with a dipping sauce of your choice (or try the Honey Mustard Sauce on page 181).

Note: When eating rattlesnake, it's best to use your fingers to pull and tear the meat away from the bones.

Adapted from the recipe by Natalie and Nic, MillennialHome steader.com

---

WINE SUGGESTION:

J. Lohr Estates Riverstone Chardonnay

The 2018 Riverstone Chardonnay exhibits youthful hues of light straw. The enticing aromas are reminiscent of white peach, apricot, ripe orange, and cocoa, and complemented by the palate flavors of citrus cream and nectarine. The rich texture and balance on the palate from aging *sur lie* gives way to flavors of vanilla, crème brûlée, and a hint of oak on the long finish.

COMMON SNAPPING TURTLE

Chelydra serpentine

The Common snapping turtle (a.k.a. snapper) is a large prehistoric reptile. It has been on the planet for 200 million years—even before the dinosaurs! It has basically remained unchanged for nearly 90 million years. The snapper's North American range covers the entire eastern United States, California, Oregon, Washington, and eastern New Mexico, Montana, and southern Canada.

The Common snapping turtle is a large, aggressive freshwater turtle. When it is out of the water, it becomes belligerent and uses its highly flexible head to inflict a lightning-quick defensive strike. It's believed to be so belligerent because it can't physically withdraw its head into its carapace (shell). The Common snapping turtle should not be confused with its larger but more docile cousin, the Alligator snapping turtle. The Common snapper is the most widespread of the two American snapping turtles. A snapper can reach the ripe old age of 100 years. Adult males can weigh more than 22 pounds, and there was once a 50-year-old snapper that weighed a record-breaking 75 pounds.

Snappers inhabit shallow ponds, streams, and brackish waters. Common snapping turtles usually lie at the water's bottom with their heads exposed to catch prey with a blinding quick strike. When they come to the surface to breathe, snappers only poke their nostrils above water to get a quick breath of air. The snapper's mouth is strong and shaped like a bird beak but it is toothless. Snappers will eat any critter they can catch and swallow. Their main diet consists of salamanders, minnows, larger fish, smaller turtles, frogs, invertebrates, snakes, birds, muskrats, and unwary ducklings. Although adult snappers have few predators, as hatchlings they are prey for racoons, fox, mink, muskrats, birds of prey, large fish and snakes, and the blue heron—I call that turn-around fair play.

Where it is legal, snappers can be hunted. Laws, season dates, and licensing requirements vary greatly from state-to-state and there are many different legal methods for harvesting turtles. Check with local game departments prior to hunting them.

One of the safest ways to catch a snapper is to use a floating trap or, better yet, a trap set up along the water's edge. There are specific traps made to catch turtles available online. Similar in method to catching blue claw crabs, tie a piece of chicken leg or some gizzards to the inside of the trap. Place the trap along the edge of the shoreline so that it is barely covered by water. It won't take long before the snapper smells the meat and takes the bait! If you don't catch a snapper within a few hours, reset the trap in another location. Snappers can also be fished for with a stout rod and reel, 50-pound test fishing line, a steel leader, and a strong small treble hook. With enough weight on a sinker, set the baited hook just above the water's bottom. Good baits include small live bluegill, chicken gizzards, a piece of meat, a few nightcrawlers, even a live minnow or sucker will do. The best bait, however, will be that with a tough consistency. Once you cast your line, set the pole in a metal rod holder placed in the ground, pull out your folding chair, and relax reading the rest of this book. Don't get too relaxed, though; it shouldn't take long to catch your snapper!

Nowadays, eating snapping turtles isn't at the top of most folks' bucket lists. But then again, if more people knew how tasty they can be when prepared correctly, they would change their tune. Turtle meat can be a mouthwatering dish when it is cleaned and cooked with a lot of care and some creative preparation. Snapper meat, like turkey and chicken, has both dark and white meat. It can be used in soup, deep-fried, grilled, and even baked. Snapper meat has been described as tasting like chicken, pork, beef, shrimp, veal, fish, and even goat. No matter the method you choose to prepare this delectable source of wild game table fare, you can be sure that the delicious meal will be accompanied by a fascinating tale of how it was sourced!

SNAPPING TURTLE SOUP

SERVES 6

3 tablespoons cooking oil

3 pounds boneless snapping turtle meat, cubed

Salt and pepper, to taste

1 large yellow onion, peeled and chopped

2–3 cloves garlic, peeled and chopped

4–5 yellow potatoes, peeled and cubed

8–10 fresh tomatoes, chopped

1 (11-ounce) can corn

Garlic powder, as needed, to taste

9 cups water or beef stock (or stock made from turtle bones)

In a large Dutch oven over high heat, add the oil. When hot, season the turtle meat with salt and pepper and add to the pot, browning on all sides. Remove the meat from the pot and set aside. Reduce the heat to low and add the onion and garlic, stirring occasionally. Cook until the onions are soft. Add the potatoes, tomatoes, corn, and the browned turtle meat. Season with garlic powder and additional salt and pepper, if necessary. Add enough water or stock to just cover the ingredients (about 9 cups). Cover and let cook at a high simmer for 45 minutes, or until the potatoes are cooked through. Remove from the stove and serve.

Note: If you prefer a thicker soup, add a slurry of water and flour and stir into the soup until desired thickness is achieved. Cook the soup for an additional 15 minutes before serving.

Adapted from the recipe by Steve on HillbillyHaven.com

WINE SUGGESTION:

J. Lohr Estates Los Osos Merlot

The 2017 J. Lohr Estates Los Osos Merlot is medium-dark in color with a mature red hue. Varietal aromas of black plum and violet meld with a barrel signature of hazelnut and brown baking spices, while the generous fraction of Malbec in the blend accentuates bright fruit tones and contributes a note of hibiscus flower. Firm tannins and lively acidity cascade to a lengthy red-fruit finish.

DEEP-FRIED SNAPPING TURTLE

SERVES 5

½ cup white vinegar

2 quarts water

Meat from 1 medium-sized
    snapping turtle

1½ cups all-purpose flour

½ cup cornmeal

2 tablespoons Cajun seasoning

1 egg, beaten

2 tablespoons water

Vegetable or peanut oil, as
    needed, for frying

Add the vinegar and water to a large heavy pot over high heat. This will help tenderize the turtle meat. Bring to a boil and add the meat. Reduce the heat to low, cover, and allow to simmer for 1 hour. Remove the meat and discard the vinegar-water. When cool to the touch, pick the turtle meat away from the bones, preferably in bite-sized pieces.

Mix the flour, cornmeal, and Cajun seasoning together in a shallow bowl. In a separate bowl, beat the egg with water to make an egg wash.

Return the pot to the stove over high heat. Add enough oil for deep-frying. Use a candy thermometer to reach 350°F.

Dip the pieces of turtle into the egg wash, then toss in the flour mixture. Allow the pieces to rest for 5 minutes to set the coating on the meat. Drop the meat into the pot, being careful not to overcrowd the pot and lower the temperature. You may need to cook in batches. Fry for 5 minutes, or until golden-brown and the turtle pieces float to the top. Remove and drain on paper towels. Serve with your favorite dipping sauce (or try the Honey Mustard Sauce on page 181).

Adapted from the recipe by Michael Pendley and RealTree.com

WINE SUGGESTION:

J. Lohr October Night Chardonnay

The 2017 October Night Chardonnay is pale straw yellow in color, with exotic floral aromas of gardenia, tangerine, baked pear, honeysuckle, and baking spices. Traditional Burgundian winemaking techniques, such as weekly stirring of the lees in French oak barrels, were used to complement these aromatics, providing a creamy palate texture. This unique Chardonnay blend provides balanced and complex flavors of ripe citrus, white peaches, and offers a hint of sweet chocolate and toasted oak on the long finish.

SNAPPING TURTLE GRAVY AND RICE

SERVES 8

½ cup cooking oil

5–6 pounds turtle meat

Creole or Cajun seasoning, to taste

½ cup flour

3 yellow onions, peeled and chopped

2 celery stalks, chopped

2 bell peppers, seeded and chopped

1 cup green onions, chopped

4 cloves garlic, peeled and minced

1 cup mushrooms, sliced

¼ cup Kitchen Bouquet (browning and seasoning sauce)

4 cups tomatoes, stewed, crushed or whole with juice

Cooked white rice, as needed

Chop the turtle meat in small pieces and season with the Creole or Cajun seasoning.

Heat a Dutch oven over high heat. Add the oil. When hot, add the turtle meat and brown on all sides. Do not crowd the pan; cook in batches if necessary. Remove the meat and set aside.

Add the flour to the pot and stir or whisk well with the oil and drippings to make a roux. When the roux is formed, add the onions, celery, bell peppers, green onions, and garlic. Cook, stirring often, until vegetables are soft. Return the browned turtle meat to the pot along with the mushrooms, Kitchen Bouquet, and tomatoes. Bring to a low boil, then reduce heat and simmer slowly for 2 ½ hours, or until the turtle meat is tender. Stir occasionally to prevent sticking. Remove from heat and serve over white rice.

Adapted from the recipe by Raschell and Misshomemade.com

WINE SUGGESTION:

J. Lohr Hilltop Cabernet Sauvignon

The 2017 J. Lohr Hiilltop Cabernet Sauvignon shows splendid ripe fruit, Cocoa powder, and graphite on the nose. The palate comes across dense chalky and soft, with layers of black currant, mineral, and notes of toasted pastry.

ACKNOWLEDGMENTS

The author would like to graciously acknowledge the following for their assistance and support with this book:

Nicole Frail and Skyhorse Publishing. Photographers Tucker + Hossler. The literary assistance of Kate Fidducia. The following representatives and wineries for their exceptional pairings: Miriam Pitt, J.A.M PR; J Lohr Vineyards, Duckhorn Vineyards; Lilja Jonsson and Ste. Michelle Wine Estates; Raquel Royers and Clos Du Val Winery; Ryan Johnson and King Estate; Alyssa Smock, Keri Tawney and DeLille Cellars; Alex Jankowski and Wagner Vineyards; Peter Heyworth and Grgich Hills; Jim and Karin Fraioli for the book's cover props; Tiffany Fraioli; Bert Clay for all the deliveries; and last, but definitely not least, all of the recipe contributors across America. Thank you.

CONVERSION CHARTS

Metric and Imperial Conversions

(These conversions are rounded for convenience)

Ingredient	Cups/Tablespoons/Teaspoons	Ounces	Grams/Milliliters
Butter	1 cup/ 16 tablespoons/ 2 sticks	8 ounces	230 grams
Cheese, shredded	1 cup	4 ounces	110 grams
Cream cheese	1 tablespoon	0.5 ounce	14.5 grams
Cornstarch	1 tablespoon	0.3 ounce	8 grams
Flour, all-purpose	1 cup/1 tablespoon	4.5 ounces/0.3 ounce	125 grams/8 grams
Flour, whole wheat	1 cup	4 ounces	120 grams
Fruit, dried	1 cup	4 ounces	120 grams
Fruits or veggies, chopped	1 cup	5 to 7 ounces	145 to 200 grams
Fruits or veggies, pureed	1 cup	8.5 ounces	245 grams
Honey, maple syrup, or corn syrup	1 tablespoon	0.75 ounce	20 grams
Liquids: cream, milk, water, or juice	1 cup	8 fluid ounces	240 milliliters
Oats	1 cup	5.5 ounces	150 grams
Salt	1 teaspoon	0.2 ounce	6 grams
Spices: cinnamon, cloves, ginger, or nutmeg (ground)	1 teaspoon	0.2 ounce	5 milliliters
Sugar, brown, firmly packed	1 cup	7 ounces	200 grams
Sugar, white	1 cup/1 tablespoon	7 ounces/0.5 ounce	200 grams/12.5 grams
Vanilla extract	1 teaspoon	0.2 ounce	4 grams

Oven Temperatures

Fahrenheit	Celsius	Gas Mark
225°	110°	¼
250°	120°	½
275°	140°	1
300°	150°	2
325°	160°	3
350°	180°	4
375°	190°	5
400°	200°	6
425°	220°	7
450°	230°	8

INDEX